MW01140977

What experts say about
"Time To Say Goodbye"

"What everyone needs to know." Bernie Siegel, M.D.,
Surgeon, Author.
"An excellent road map for decisions that affect all of us."
Sheldon Burchman, M.D., *Assistant Professor of Anesthesiology &
Director of Pain Management at Wisconsin Medical College, & Woods
Veterans Hospital, Milwaukee.*
"Well written. It will definitely help those for whom it is
targeted." Brian P. Buggy, M.D., *Clinical Professor of Medicine,
Medical College of Wisconsin & Infectious Disease Specialist in private
practice.*
"The ground you cover is so critical, and really missing as a
resource to patients, their families, and caregivers." Ellen
Cohen, MSW, *Director of Kenneth B. Schwartz Center established to
promote compassionate care in medical settings. Boston Massachusetts.*
"I love this book. It belongs in every home in America. I
will continue to recommend it to my listeners." Frances
Halpern, *Talk Show Host of PBS "Connections" and former book review
editor for the Los Angeles Times, Santa Barbara, California.*
"Not only a practical book, but a sensitive outline of what
needs to be done by those of us who are dying." Mary Ann
Lorentz, RN BSN, *Director of Cancer Outreach, St. Mary's
Hospital/Hospice, Milwaukee, Wisconsin.*
"The book is really quite wonderful. I know that reading it
will make a difference in people's lives." Judith Skretny,
MA, PhD candidate; *Director, Life Transitions Center, Inc., Buffalo,
New York.*
"An incredible piece! I would recommend this to patients,
families, and caregivers alike." Eileen Jaskolski, *VP of Mission
Services & Director of Pastoral Care Services, Columbia/St. Mary's
Hospitals, Milwaukee.*

ACKNOWLEDGMENTS

I am deeply grateful for the ongoing help of my husband, Harry, throughout the writing of this book, and for the support of my children, especially their generosity in allowing me to reveal the struggles and inspirations we shared as a family. A warm thank you to Frances Halpern and all of my friends and teachers at the Santa Barbara Writers Conference who spurred me on with guidance and encouragement.

I am very much indebted to my many friends and colleagues who consented to read, edit, or contribute to this work; including Rabbi Zalman Schachter-Shalomi, Professor of NAROPA Institute, Boulder, Colorado; and Judith Skretny, director of the Life Transitions Center in Buffalo.

I will always be grateful to my first hospice director, Dr. Sheldon Burchman who instilled in us all, his outstanding pain management techniques; and to Dr. Brian Buggy for his invaluable information and insight into treatment and care of the incurably ill. Many thanks to Ellen Cohen, President and co-founder of the Massachusetts based Kenneth B. Schwartz Center for the advancement of compassionate care in medical settings, who shared with us her husband, Kenneth's, story.

A profound thank you to Dr. Bernie Siegel for writing an introduction to my book; and for the kind words of Bishop Richard Sklba, Eileen Jaskolski, and Mary Ann Lorentz.

A special thank you to my son, Michael, a professional artist, who designed my cover and added the many beautiful illustrations.

It is impossible to list all those who allowed me to take part in their lives during their times of illness, sorrow, learning and growth. My most heartfelt thanks goes to these wonderful people for all they taught me, and for the times when they per-mitted me to teach them.

Time To Say Goodbye

A Guide to Empowerment During Illness & Aging

By Barbara Olive RN

Barbara Olive

Published by Lemieux International, Ltd.
P.O. Box 17134
Milwaukee, Wisconsin 53217-0134
Cover design and illustrations by Michael Olive
Manufactured in the United States of America
Library of Congress Catalogue Card Number 98-67916

ISBN: 0-9667269-0-1

Certain names and places have been
changed to protect the confidentiality
of individuals without distorting
the reality of the experience.
The author is not an attorney. Please
consult your attorney for further
legal questions or when preparing
any document that requires the force of law.

1st Printing October 1998
2nd Printing September 1999

CONTENTS

Contents

Contents

Contents

Foreword

The book is a truly lovely work of art, filled with an air of calm confidence, profound compassion and understanding. I found myself thinking that you must be a wonderful kind of Mother Image ... and instinctively liking you a great deal!

I read the entire manuscript, partially because religion and faith cannot be easily compartmentalized into merely a few pages or paragraphs of reference ... and partially because I enjoyed reading your words and sharing your wisdom. Your advice has been alchemized by your own sorrows in the deaths of your sons, and made very valuable indeed.

This is a wonderful reflection, and I know it will be immensely helpful to any and all who are blessed by having it in hand or apron pocket for the long journey home!

Most Reverend Richard J. Sklba,
Auxiliary Bishop of the
Milwaukee Archdiocese

Introduction

by Bernie Siegel, M.D.

. . The problem is, we are not educated as people or professionals. We are informed. Information can be overlooked or disregarded, except for the one thing you have learned from, our mortality.

The title of your book should read, "Time to Say Goodbye: What Everyone Needs to Know". We all have a life-threatening illness, and it is "Time". So take time to say, "I love you," to yourself and others. Learn about understanding, joyfulness, healing, and what makes life meaningful.

As soon as you accept your mortality you start to live. That's why God let Adam and Eve eat from the tree of knowledge; to learn they were mortal.

Peace.

Preface
The Choices We Face

The events that led me to the writing of this book are not the singular incidents of one American family. They are real life dramas played out quietly in millions of homes throughout the world. They are the silent backdrop to the handful of tragedies documented in daily newspapers and flashed across the six o'clock news.

Within the space of twenty-seven months, my mother succumbed to congestive heart failure, my first-born son committed suicide, and my youngest son was killed instantly in a drunk driving accident. Sitting in a workshop at the annual Santa Barbara Writers Conference, sharing pages of my grief-saturated journal, I was unaware that before the year's end my husband would suffer a heart attack.

Hovering over his gurney in the Emergency Room, I braced myself for another loss. Quick action and longevity in his genes pulled him through. By the time he was out of danger my vision cleared and I recalled warning symptoms I should have recognized, saw therapeutic steps we could have taken, preparations we ought to have made, and coping skills we might have shored up for such an emergency.

That vision changed the literary focus of my writing. I felt obligated to warn everyone that the garment of tissue that houses our being is fragile. There may come a time when it will only support our life on earth with complex medical interventions and prudent changes in lifestyle. We may find we need expanding faith and courage to carry us through one day at a time. Yet, this vision is not reason for depression, despair, or burying our heads in the sands of distractions. We can take heart from those who have not only survived the valleys of tragedy, but have prevailed by turning them into pinnacles of success and unimaginable joy. We can find out how to make their success stories our own no matter what life sends our way.

Additionally, we can pass the secrets of our acquired success to our offspring, our students, and our peers. We can support them as they pass through their own dark tunnels of sickness, loss and grief. If we find ourselves responsible for taking care of others who are ill; our aging parents, grandparents, or siblings, we will have new-found skills ready at our compassionate fingertips, and we will know how to care for those we love.

There is no one 'best way' to live through grief, loss, aging or illness; nor to prepare ourselves and others for living creatively and comfortably throughout all the times and circumstances of life. Every situation is different and each individual must find his or her own best way. Whether you are in the prime of health, are feeling the infirmities of aging, or are laboring under a severe medical diagnosis, now is the time to give some thought to your 'best way' to fill every day of your journey with joy and fulfillment.

During twenty-three years of professional nursing I witnessed the disastrous outcome of those who drifted aimlessly through illness, aging, or approaching death. Four years as a pool nurse working in a dozen local hospitals and nursing homes, showed me every possible scenario in the ongoing struggle to maintain and revive the physical functions of our human bodies; and also, many times, the irreversible decline and collapse of all bodily systems.

There were deaths under garish lights, strung with tubes and bleeping monitors, death surrounded by machines and technicians. Frigid deaths that left me chilled and nauseous. Then, the old ones in quiet lonely rooms, with pain in their bodies and fear in their eyes, as life slipped away. I remember Teddy, my cancer riddled patient, and Louise with her failing kidneys, drawing their last breath which forced me to sound the alarm. The code team rushed in to trounce on them, insert tubes, and shock them, attempting to restore their last thread of life for a few more days --- or hours. It sickened me, but I had to follow doctor's orders and abide by hospital policy.

These, and hundreds of thousands like them, were the unfortunate ones who were ravaged or ignored by medical technology. They had given no previous thought to their time to say goodbye. They didn't know when to choose going "gently into that good night" or when to "rage against the dying of the light". They didn't even know they had a choice.

We do have choices, and there are better ways. I have gathered into this book, all I've learned about the surest and wisest paths to follow to meet every health challenge we encounter. With this guide we will all be able to make our own informed choices with a minimum of fear, pain, and confusion. Through supportive preparations for the potential needs of illness and aging, we can reach our goals of joy and fulfillment for all our days, and attain the peace of a love-filled and comfortable passage across life's threshold.

* * *

The chapters are arranged in the order that problems are frequently experienced. For a quick answer to a current problem refer to the Table of Contents in the front, or the chapter summaries and index in the back. At the end of each chapter I've included a list of suggested reading for those who would like to delve into some topics in more depth. Many of them contain shared learning experiences of other persons who traveled this road before us. I've also listed names, addresses, phone numbers, and websites of health organizations, support groups, helplines, and hotlines, which you can contact for additional assistance.

Chapter I
Life's Timetable

During the years following the unexpected loss of two of our sons, my husband and I saw a surge of ambition in our remaining children. Their glimpse of life's borders intensified their goals for the here and now. Our oldest daughter cut her hours of factory work and returned to school to secure a degree in Nuclear Engineering. Another daughter switched to part time at her bank job and earned a Masters Degree in Education for the Learning Disabled. Our daughter, who was already a Respiratory Therapist, went back to school and obtained a Degree in Clinical Psychology. They did all of this while paying their own way, plus caring for their homes and children.

Our awareness of the suddenness with which someone's death could overtake us, intensified the value of our present moments. All of our lives seemed more precious. Our appreciation of each other, and our inclination to communicate honestly and more frequently, improved dramatically. Being aware that those we love could depart this world at any time prompted us to turn off the TV and talk to each other. Then we would listen to what was going on in everyone's life. Really listen, so we could discern what was going on in their hearts. We weren't so reluctant to say, "I'm sorry," or, "I love you," or, "I'm proud of you." We learned to support one another, and how to hug each other, especially when saying goodbye.

Since those days, we have not been able to keep our mortality buried under layers of denial. Considering death as an ever-present possibility kept us from wasting time worrying about the past and making interminable plans for the years ahead. It has been sufficient to map out our goals for a reasonably fulfilling future, and then set about living in the present.

* * *

It is wise to ponder the fact that accidents, disasters, and sudden illness do happen, and that what we are doing now may be our last activity. We'll make sure it's something worth while and pay attention to the pleasure and fulfillment it offers. Realizing the uncertainties that hang on the edges our lives can open us to following our dreams. Insofar as it does not involve abandoning our responsibilities to family and society, we can begin taking more risks, make a career change, apply for that new job, go back to school, start our own business, learn a new language. try bungee jumping, or go back-packing through Europe. Then, as peak performers, the majority of us will spiral to maturity and the fullness of life.

TIME TO SAY GOODBYE

If we could choose the ideal final chapter to our life, most of us would plan on being healthy and active long into our senior years and then, without even thinking about it, go quickly, preferably while in our sleep. Modern technology, however, has found ways to keep our bodies going with powerful medications, treatments, surgery, and resuscitation, so fewer people than ever before in history will get their wish for an instantaneous death.

Working in the hospice, preparing some of our growing numbers of aged and incurably ill patients for their passage over life's threshold, convinced me of the advantages of having this prolonged time of farewell. I realized that it would actually provide the most fulfilling closure to my own life. I'm going to need this time to get my papers in order, consider what I've done with my life, make amends for sloughing off at times, do what I really want to accomplish in the time left, exchange heartfelt words with my family, my friends, and God, and then say goodbye. Put that way it doesn't sound so bad, does it?

During the last fifty years, this prolonged extension of life in our culture has become recognized as the norm. Sociologists and psychologists now identify it as a separate developmental stage which provides an opportunity for the completion of our personal growth. It is our final chance to reach the peak of human achievement and perfection. A prime example of this is the modern artist, Monet, who painted four hundred fifty of his finest works between the age of sixty-five and eighty-six, during declining health and impaired vision.

Many of us will slip into this extended life period gradually, as passing years take their toll on our bodies. Long before my petite mother-in-law, known by the French diminutive, "Memere" by all the family, reached her ninety-eighth birthday, she had lost most of her sight and hearing. Arthritic joints forced her to move very slowly and only with a walker. A failing immune system brought on frequent bladder and respiratory infections. Small strokes (now called "brain accidents") left her intermittently confused.

She prevailed over her declining health with a stubbornness that proved to be her best and worst trait during the years she made her home with us. She never refused an invitation to a party and was passionate about playing and winning at Bridge. By the time her body's systems gave out, she had said her goodbyes, and looked forward to moving on.

Officially, in our present hi-tech medical world, no one is allowed to die of old age. To make a report legal, a coroner must declare a specific cause of death, often pneumonia or heart failure. A physician would be reprimanded by his colleagues should he write "Old Age" as the primary cause on a death certificate. However, barring accident or incurable illness, when enough of our body parts wear out, and no medical intervention can repair them, we die of old age.

THE DIAGNOSIS

For some the awareness of life's limitations comes suddenly, in the form a physician's diagnosis. Bear in mind that no diagnosis eliminates room for hope. Much of what takes place in our bodies is still mystery to even the most brilliant physicians. The challenge may begin when your doctor tells you that what you thought was the flu, bronchitis, a stiff neck, or a skin rash, is actually an incurable virus, or an inoperable cancer. After hearing your doctor's report, your first reaction will shoot off in one of these ways:

Your heart will sink, your body feel like lead, and your mind will blur, but deep down somewhere you'll believe it's true. You know this doctor and have implicit faith in his care for you; you've also been feeling poorly for some time; you've been exposed to a contagious disease; the pain is getting worse; or you are weaker this month than last month.

Even though you acknowledge that what your doctor is telling you is the truth, it is still a shock, and after hearing this 'sentence' you won't remember much of whatever else the doctor is saying. It is the most devastating news anyone can hear in their lifetime, especially heartbreaking for those in their prime with much left to do, perhaps with young children to raise.

Another way of reacting to a diagnosis like this is: "There's got to be some mistake. Are you sure those tests are conclusive?" The doctor will go on to explain the facts and you will counter with, "There must be something we can do to cure this." Some deep-seated instinct inside you keeps telling you this can't be true, this can't be happening to you. This is a common reaction if you've been active and feeling pretty well up till now.

What you are experiencing is what some call 'denial' the first stage of grief, which is actually a psychological self-defense mechanism. Our minds and bodies cannot handle a sudden life-threatening blow of this magnitude in one stroke. We need time to work into it gradually.

It's also a form of self-defense because we want to be absolutely sure that our illness is, in fact, incurable. Whichever way you react to your diagnosis, don't make any hasty decisions. Go home, give yourself time to think about this. If you are not completely convinced that this doctor, these diagnostic tests, or those X-Rays, are correct, it is your right to get a second opinion, and another if need be.

Demand to see copies of your tests, review them with specialists in this field, and copy down the results for yourself. Do research at your library, or contact the national society for your particular disease be it cancer, Acquired Immune Deficiency Syndrome, Amyotrophic Lateral Sclerosis, Rheumatoid Arthritis, or whatever, to get all the information available on your illness. This may sound drastic, but tragic mistakes have been made, and you don't want to be one of them. During recent years I've consistently heard stories about, and personally witnessed, mis-diagnosed and mismanaged diseases.

A HEALTH PARTNER

If you are a person who readily shares with others all that is going on in your life, you've probably told your friends and loved ones you haven't been feeling well, then filled them in with your doctor's report and everything you've encountered thus far. Ask one of them to help as you review your test results and do some research to ferret out the truth about your illness.

It would be wise to have this person accompany you on your next visit to the physician's office because it's extremely difficult for you to concentrate on the facts at this time. You need a caring partner to go with you, ask questions, and take notes. "Health Partners" ought to have at least a little spare time to devote to this, so tell them ahead of time what you are going to need.

A health partner is a valuable asset in getting the best out of your personal health care. Today's medical system is not always 'user friendly' because health insurance companies and Medicare insist on keeping it 'cost effective'. The fewer diagnostic tests and treatments each patient receives, the smaller are the expenses and the greater the profit. This 'minimalist' system has resulted in many missed diagnoses, untreated illnesses, unnecessary pain and suffering, and even death. If your health partner is sitting next to you in a doctor's office, clinic, or hospital, assiduously taking notes and asking questions, your doctor, nurse, or therapist will make doubly sure that the tests, treatments, and medications prescribed are thorough and correct.

Several years ago my husband began suffering with stiff and painful joints. After several weeks of discomfort he saw his usual primary physician, who told him it was normal to experience aches and pains at his age. He prescribed Ibubrofen to relieve the symptoms. I was furious when my husband told me this because I know aches and pains are not normal at any age. I held my peace and hoped he would recover. Two weeks later the pain was getting so bad he couldn't eat, sleep, or reach up into the cupboard for a coffee cup. "Make another appointment," I told him, "and this time I'll go with you."

I got out my AMA Home Medical Advisor and looked up his symptoms. They indicated that he might have Rheumatoid Arthritis, Lyme's Disease, Lupus, or Degenerative Joint Disease. I checked my old nursing books to see what appropriate lab tests would identify these diseases. Armed with this information we visited the doctor.

I saw that part of the problem was the vague manner in which my husband spoke to the doctor. "I'm not doing so good," was all he volunteered. It is essential to describe all complaints and difficulties specifically, including what your pain feels like, where it is, and how severe it feels. Be as accurate in describing your bodily complaints as you are in describing your car's jerks, knocks, and pings to your auto mechanic.

The doctor increased the dose of Ibuprofen and was about to send my husband on his way, when I jumped in with my list of possible diseases and their accompanying lab tests. The doctor got on the phone immediately and made an appointment with a Rheumatologist. With proper treatment my husband recovered in six weeks.

* * *

If you feel uneasy about any aspect of your health care, insist on reading your chart. Every person has a legal right to review his or her own chart at any time, and if your health partner is with you, you can view the information together. If you don't understand the medical terminology ask your doctor to explain it. It is every health provider's duty, not only to care for you, but to enlist your cooperation in the healing process by giving you clear explanations and a thorough understanding of instructions.

* * *

Many people prefer to keep quiet about their diagnosis at this stage so as not to worry anyone needlessly. If you have always felt more comfortable absorbing information into yourself and dealing with it on your own terms, you will do that, and tell family and friends later. You will find the going easier if you have at least one trusted friend or relative with whom to talk over the medical advice you are receiving, and assist you with additional research on your disease. A health partner can give you objective opinions or simply hear you out as you discuss your problems.

Your spouse or significant other may be too emotionally involved to be level-headed at this time, only you can be the judge of that. It might be better to choose someone else whom you feel comfortable talking to, someone you are sure can keep a secret. They can help you find the right words to say to your family when you are ready to tell them about your illness. Unless you leave town or have some secluded hideaway, you will have to tell them eventually, because your physical and mental distress will become more and more obvious.

THE RIGHT TREATMENTS

It may be that after more consults, tests, and research you become aware that your condition is getting worse. A growing conviction in your mind and in your heart tells you that you do have a life-threatening illness, and your best course of action will be treatments to slow its progress, negate its effects on your body, and hopefully cure you. There are usually several types of treatments available for the major illnesses such as cancers, AIDS, kidney dysfunction, liver disease, ALS, multiple sclerosis, and heart disease.

When Joanne, who was in her late forties, found she had breast cancer, she opted for a mastectomy at a cost of about $6,000. She followed this with six months of chemotherapy and five weeks of radiation for an additional $14,000. Her medical insurance covered all but $10 co-pay for each doctor visit, $250 co-pay for inpatient hospitalization, and $4 co-pay for each month's supply of oral medication.

Completing the above course of action cut nearly one full year out of her life. After recovering from surgery, for six months she reported to her hospital once every two weeks for a doctor's exam, blood tests, and intravenous chemotherapy infusion. During the interim she took oral chemotherapy medication. She felt tired during these months, felt grieved at losing her thick, black hair, but otherwise had no ill effects, and she did not find the regimen too disagreeable. A month later she started on five weeks of radiation which required her to go to her hospital every weekday for one-half hour treatments. Again she complained of tiredness, but no other symptoms.

It's too early to tell if the surgery and treatments were completely successful, but Joanne feels well, and is confident about her recovery. She says that surgery and the follow-up treatments were definitely worth her time, effort, and money.

For your condition you will need detailed information on what each treatment entails in terms of side effects, cost, length of time it takes to complete, and whether or not you must be hospitalized during the process. Some treatments may require you to spend five weeks in an intensive care unit at a cost of $80,000. Some are available only at specialized clinics in other states. You must part with your loved ones and reside at the clinic for several weeks or months.

Find out how much of an improvement or longevity the treatment can provide for you. What percentage of success has it met with in other patients? Have your doctor clarify what success means for you in your present condition. Does it mean a total cure, or an increased life span of three months, twelve months, or two years? Will you feel well again, or have an increase in physical mobility and mental clarity? Does success mean it will eliminate your pain or decrease your dependency on others?

If your doctor won't answer these questions you can do research on your own or contact one of the supportive organizations for your health problem listed at the back of this book.

If you are satisfied with the prospects of this treatment, there is still the percentage rate to consider. If forty per cent of those treated received all of the maximum benefits, you may want to consider it. Remember that sixty per cent did not benefit, and some died during treatment. If only five per cent met with success, you may not want to risk the time, discomfort, or money.

For any treatment or surgery you decide on, especially if your condition is unusual or complicated, find a doctor who does at least thirty such procedures a year. Find a hospital or clinic that specializes in your condition. Statistics show that specialty facilities and doctors who perform the greatest number of specialized procedures have the highest success rate. Doctors themselves recommend that if your request for a specialist is denied, be tenacious, persistent and pushy.

Don't let yourself be pressured into making a decision about any particular treatment. Unless you have a type of cancer that grows rapidly, such as a lymphoma, a few weeks time in deciding won't make your situation more critical. Weigh all the in-formation you receive until you feel satisfied in choosing the right treatment. It is a rare situation that can't wait at least a few days. If your treatments involve signing a consent form, take a copy of it home to study before signing. Read it carefully so you don't consign yourself to procedures you don't want. Some consent forms give the doctors blanket permission to do anything they want while you are admitted to their care.

Make sure you have a doctor you can talk to freely and comfortably, one that will take time to answer your questions, giving you precise and prompt explanations of tests and treatments. Doctors have been trained to cure every patient under their care. Many are still struggling with their own helplessness when faced with an incurable disease, and with their own personal concerns about end of life care. Doctors who are committed to curing, but not caring for their patients, find subtle ways to abandon those who don't adhere to their rules.

If anything strikes you as phony or uncaring during your interactions with your doctor, even if it is only an indefinable uneasiness, confront him with your observation. If he takes offense or is unwilling to cooperate with you, find a new physician. Be wary of the physician who proposes his choice of treatment as the only way to save your life, or tells you it is experimental but what have you got to lose.

Before you leave the doctor's office, verbally review his instructions and the information he has given you to make sure you have them right. Here is where your health partner will be invaluable in keeping accurate notes and asking questions.

It's wise to prepare a list of questions and concerns before your next visit. It's helpful to have a 'Visit to the Doctor' notebook containing your questions and your doctor's explanations and instructions. At the front of this notebook leave a couple of pages for names, addresses, and phone numbers of any therapists, clinics, or specialists he refers you to.   Then leave a few pages to list your present medications with their strengths, dosages, and comments.   When you change a medication, cross out the old one and add the new one at the bottom of the list.   If your health partner can't be with you to take notes, bring along a tape recorder so you can review the entire visit later.

Medical personnel and caregivers have the habit of talking 'over' patients and making decisions for them, as if they weren't there or had no minds of their own. Don't hesitate to interrupt those who treat you in this manner.   You will manage your illness more to your satisfaction if you take charge of it from the beginning.

IT'S YOUR DECISION

You'll incorporate the ideas and feelings that feedback from your health partner gives you, but this is your body and your life, so you must make the final decisions.   Ask your health partner to stand by you if others don't agree with your choices.   Standing up for what you want can become very difficult when your loved ones try hard to dissuade you.   Be prepared.

If you decide at some point that the treatment you've chosen isn't helping, discuss your feelings with your physician.   You are not committed to following through with it on blind faith, and your doctor will want to know how it is affecting you.   He or she may want to try something else.

* * *

Most doctors will not object to your using one of the complementary physical treatments available such as acupuncture, massage, reiki, or acupressure, but make certain your doctor is aware of this. These treatments of your choice can enhance your feeling of well-being, while you do something positive to promote your own healing. Keep in mind that if one of these complementary treatments were a cure, everyone would be using it. They have been found to be most effective in conjunction with traditional medical practice. Again, tell your doctor before you start these.

Substances taken internally such as herbs, special diets, or untested remedies, can interfere with your prescription medications or otherwise adversely affect your system.   Don't take anything into your body unless your doctor specifically okays it. If there is an herbal remedy which particularly appeals to you, have your doctor check it in the most complete modern guide to herbal remedies, their drug interactions, and contraindications, the "Commission E Monoghaph" which is the official research and guide approved by the German government. You can do the research yourself in your local library, but talk with your doctor before taking anything.

* * *

Some individuals who are newly diagnosed with a life-threatening illness that may or may not become terminal, decide that lengthy and disagreeable treatments would add further distress to the time they have left. They seem to have an inner conviction pointing them in this direction. Others are prepared to fight their disease with every means available. What do you strongly believe in your head and feel intuitively in your heart? Only you can discern which path you want to follow. Don't be pressured into doing what you don't feel is right for you just to satisfy someone else.

Some people do choose to forego treatments, and to avoid conflicts 'disappear' from family and society. Ruth was seventy-one years old, a widow, who was diagnosed with lung cancer. She felt she had lived a full life and was ready to join her husband in the next, so she refused any treatments. Except for the housekeeper who lived with her, she told no one about her cancer and gradually cut herself off from the outside world. When she could no longer live alone she entered a hospice, and died with the companionship of a few caregivers. Ruth was a quiet, dignified woman who did not wish to distress or trouble anyone, and she believed to the end that this was the 'best' way for her.

If you have a nagging conscience telling you that it's your duty to stay alive for your children, spouse, lover, or parents, you may find yourself suffering through treatments with growing resentments and internal conflicts. The solution lies in discussing these feelings with your physician, minister, or counselor; then drawing out into the open, the thoughts and feelings of everyone involved by means of the honest, straightforward communication described in chapter three.

* * *

Whether our own life's timetable presents us with the slowly increasing difficulties of aging, or strikes us with the sudden jolt of serious accident or illness, most of us try several coping strategies before finding those that work well. Our first reactions may be to:
- wallow in self-pity.
- displace our anger and take it out on everyone around us.
- give up hope of any healing or happiness and become an invalid long before it's necessary.
- avoid the struggle by attempting suicide, assisted or otherwise.

With guidance, persistence, and prayer we can begin to discard the tactics that increase our distress, and discover ways to:
- use this time to live more fully than we ever have before, the way we would have lived all along if we'd known the end would come this soon.

- take stock of our possibilities and our limitations and meet the problem as another of life's challenges we must face up to.
- use this time to put our house in order, and complete our inner journey.
- give our loved ones a chance to learn and grow along with us.

Additional Reading

Patricia Weenolsen, "The Art of Dying", St. Martin Press, NY 1996.

Bernie Siegel, "Love, Medicine, and Miracles", Harper Row, NY, 1986.

Elisabeth Kubler-Ross, "On Death and Dying", Macmillan Publishers, N.Y., 1969.

The American Medical Association (AMA) Home Medical Guide, Random House, N.Y., 1982, also in the reference section of your local library.

Joanne Lynn MD, "Handbook for Mortals: Guidance for People Facing Serious Illness", Oxford Press, N.Y. 1999.

To check Board Certification of a Specialist call:
American Board of Medical Specialties,
800-776-CERT (9am to 6pm)
These doctors must have 3-7 years training in their
specialty plus pass the Board exam.

William Collinge, M.P.H.,P.H.D., "The American
Holistic Health Association Complete Guide to
Alternative Medicine." Warner Books, Inc. NY, 1996

✓ Commission E Monograph, official publication of the
German Government for herbal remedies, herb contra-
indications and drug interactions.
Available in the reference section of your local library.

Richard Walters, "Options: Alternative Therapies for
Cancer Patients", Avery Publishing Group.

Linda Rector Page, N.D. Ph.D., "Healthy Healing",
Healthy Healing Publications.

Resource for publications about complementary and
alternative medicine research supported by NIH:
OAM Clearinghouse - Office of Alternative Medicine,
National Institute of Health. P.O. Box 8218,
Silver Spring, Maryland 20907-8218.   888-644-6226.

Chapter II
Living With A Life-Threatening Illness

You have accepted the fact that your doctor was right about your diagnosis, and may have come to realize that treatments are not curing your illness. You are forced to face the truth that you may not have much time left. Perhaps your doctor told you how much time that will be, but those predictions are seldom accurate.

HOW LONG DO I HAVE?

At family gatherings my Aunt Leone loved to tell the story of her 'terminal' illness. Hospitalized in midlife, her doctor diagnosed her with a severe hypertensive disease, and told her to put her affairs in order because she could go at any time. Through surgery and a regime of medications she lived another thirty years.

Her punchline was: the doctor who diagnosed her had died many years ago. Her secret was: for thirty years she remained aware that she could go at any time. On the roulette wheel of life, chances for the sick and the healthy may be about the same. The difference is in awareness.

During my years as a Hospice nurse I was frequently confronted by patients and their families with the question, "How much longer do we have?" At first I gave them a time based on the doctor's opinion and on the patient's physical symptoms. I was invariably wrong and had to make excuses which irritated everyone. I soon learned the truth and told them simply, "We don't know for sure." This answer did not satisfy them either. For some reason it would have been easier if I could have said, "two weeks from today at 4:32 a.m.".

I assisted a woman with lung cancer through a bronchoscopy exam in which a scope was inserted through her bronchial tubes to the entrance of her right lung. I viewed the damage the growing tumor had done to that lung and when I heard the doctor say she had about two weeks to live, I believed him. When the doctor told this to the woman, whose name was Shirley, she lashed out at him angrily. "How dare you tell me how long I have to live? I'm going to beat this cancer, and you're going to help me." Shirley found the best radiologist in her home town and followed radiation with chemotherapy. She lived a fairly comfortable life in her own home, with her husband and visiting nurses caring for her, for two and one-half years.

If Shirley had been of a more passive nature, she would have accepted the doctor's opinion and returned home to die. Predictions based on statistics and physical findings don't take into account the amount of hope and determination in each person's heart. The sheer will to live is a powerful healer.

When congestive heart failure, a slow deterioration of the heart muscle, left my eighty-two year old mother too weak to live alone, my husband and I took her into our home. With the help of visiting nurses and aides, a physical therapist, portable oxygen therapy, and a rented hospital bed, we managed well for seven months. I remember clearly the day the visiting nurse updated me on my mother's condition and said, "She's doing well. She could go on like this for another year." Mother, however, had grown weary of the daily tedium of keeping herself alive. She died the next day. Another lesson for me that the time allotted to each of us is notoriously unpredictable.

COMBATING EARLY DEPRESSION

Depressive thoughts, feelings of sadness, and hopelessness can begin to attack you as soon as you can no longer effectively deny the seriousness of your situation. This early depression is a direct reaction to the consequences of illness or the effects of aging.

Perhaps you have now had a recurrence of symptoms, and have had to re-enter the hospital for further surgery or treatments. The surgery can be painful and disfiguring, and even with medical insurance, it can pose a great financial burden on you and your family. You see your spouse or other family members paying bills and shouldering responsibilities that you feel should be rightfully yours.

In chapter six you'll find out how and where to get help with your physical and financial burdens. What is important now is that you avoid sinking into a depressive state that will weigh you and your family with additional burdens. You can take steps now to maintain your highest quality of life for the time that remains.

MAINTAINING A HEALTHY OUTLOOK

Remember, we are all dying in some manner so instead of thinking of yourself as dying, or as good as dead, mentally reinforce the fact that you are still very much alive. With all that is going on in your life you will find that you're living more intensely than when you thought your time was limitless.

Don't hesitate to talk about your illness, in your own mind now, and with others as soon as you are ready. Call it by name, because trying to hide it will not make it go away and will prevent you from learning some of the most important lessons life has yet to offer. Don't, however, think and talk about nothing but your illness. Replaying in your mind and with others a continuous stream of each symptom, pain, or new medication that has entered your life, will drive others away, and shrivel what remains of your zest for living.

There is a way to reach a healthy balance between accepting your disease, taking care of yourself, and making plans for the time you have left; with alternating periods of time in which you forget about your illness, and enjoy what you are doing at the moment. If negative thoughts invade your mind during interludes of enjoyment such as, "I shouldn't be happy, I'm dying.", replace them with a positive thought.

Positive thoughts include, "I will have many enjoyable moments doing the things I like," or "I deserve to be happy while I'm alive." It is just as hurtful to deny yourself the pleasures of living as it is to avoid confronting the fact that you do have a life-threatening illness.

With a little practice you can catch any negative thoughts that creep in at this time. Some don't just creep, they overwhelm you with feelings of loss, failure, and guilt. Thinking of yourself as defenseless against your illness with thoughts like, "There's no hope for me. There's nothing I can do about this." Or, "I might as well be dead already.", will defeat you. Acknowledge that you have negative thoughts and then purge them from your mind.

Indulging in negative thinking will prevent you from living with the best feelings, the most enjoyment, and with the continuing social and intimate relationships to which you are entitled. If morbid brooding starts to slide you down into depression, turn your attention to a beautiful sight, a garden, a painting, or a memory. Have a humorous book handy to lift your spirits. Dive into an enjoyable pastime, or a favorite hobby. Exercising your positive outlook is as valuable an activity as exercising your body.

STIGMA

If your disease is causing visible disability or disfigurement you may feel like an eyesore among healthy individuals and want to hide away. Keep an image of yourself in your mind's eye of the beautiful person you really are, with all your knowledge, accomplishments, and loving relationships. Enhance your self image by saying and thinking to yourself, "I am not my disease. I am much more than my body. I am a unique, irreplaceable person."

You will grieve if you are still youthful and find you are no longer sexually attractive to others. Or you may be experiencing a difficult sexual relationship with your loved one. Explore other means of continuing a loving sexual relationship by means of touching, massaging, cuddling, and caressing.

Others with disfiguring illnesses or handicaps have found that it helps to 'not notice' for the few minutes that passers-by stare at them. When the strangers' curiosity is satisfied they go on about their business. Letting them 'look' gives other people a chance to contemplate a different kind of body, wondering what it must feel like, wondering how you deal with it. It gives them pause to think about the fact that it could have been their body. The insightful begin to wonder how they would handle it if, indeed, it might someday be their body.

Your family and close friends will scarcely notice the progression of changes in your appearance. To them you will be the same person you always were, a little weaker, more needful of their help perhaps, but still you.

A sense of humor is invaluable for achieving a healthy outlook through all of this. When my uncle learned he had to have his left leg amputated he remarked, "Keep an eye out for some fellow without his right leg. I've got some great left shoes to give him." The day before his surgery he wrote a poem called, "By Bits and Pieces":

> Some problems rise of different sorts,
> We cannot ask for less or more;
> Some people leave with all their parts,
> But others send some on before.

> Decisions made that I should leave,
> Observing some installment plan,
> Are not sufficient cause to grieve,
> But just the lot of mortal man.

YOUR ILLNESS AS CHALLENGE

You can redefine your illness by viewing it as a challenge. You have met and overcome other challenges in your life and you can be successful in:

* * *

- taking charge of and managing this disease.
- keeping pain and symptoms under control.
- putting financial and business affairs in order.
- arranging for necessary medical and nursing care.
- deepening relationships.
- strengthening family ties.
- developing your spiritual awareness.
- completing or beginning creative projects.
- finding enjoyable activities with family and friends.

This is a sample of the goals you can strive for. You can probably think of more. Make a list of them and keep them handy to reinforce positive thoughts.

MEDITATION

If you are in the habit of getting in touch with your spiritual center through prayer, spiritual reading, and meditation, you have an additional healing tool at your disposal. You may find your focus shifting to mortality, suffering, or the life to come. Answers to the deeper meanings of life and death may begin to unfold. Use your meditation time for enlightenment, and to get away from daily cares. It is the time to quiet your mind and relax your body.

If you're not familiar with these methods, there are booklets of spiritual reflections in different faiths to help you get started. Prayer is talking to God, meditation is resting in His presence and listening, although the two often intertwine.

If you find your spiritual reflections interrupted by angry thoughts about your illness, such as, "Why did God do this to me?" Tell God whatever is in your mind and heart. That is prayer. God is big enough to handle your anger. For additional help with this problem see ANGER AT GOD in Chapter Eight.

BODILY CONSIDERATION

Your body used to be your obedient servant, one that required care so basic you rarely thought about it. Through pain and other disagreeable symptoms, your body is now demanding an outrageous amount of attention. So much so, that you have had to change your lifestyle.

If you find yourself saying something like, "Why did that damned foot have to swell up so much I can't put my shoe on?", you need some positive thinking exercises to draw you away from self-hatred. Try saying instead, "Poor foot, you carried me around for years, now I'm going to take care of you."

Visualize your body as a faithful friend who is sick and needs your help. Imagine how you'd react to a sick child with a swollen foot, or to your afflicted dog or cat. Your body needs the same kindness and compassion you would show to them.

When Saint Francis of Assisi lay dying, he apologized to his body, which he called "Brother Ass", for the harsh treatment he inflicted on it during his lifetime. If you have been harsh with your body in the past, now is the time for tender, loving care. This includes eating nutritious food, getting sufficient rest, and exercising to the extent that you are able.

A NEW WAY OF LIFE

It is during this time of life that daily frets and tasks of the past seem to become unimportant. The demands of the ego to keep up our image, the need to support or care for our families, succeed in business, or excel in sports, all begin to fall away and we discover what really matters. Quality of life is different for each individual, so ponder what it is you most want to do with the capabilities you have now.

Some of our Hospice residents found pleasure in corresponding with old friends, others began reading books they had put aside till they had more time, one woman composed poetry, and an elderly gentleman began writing his memoirs. Many of our residents enjoyed recording their life story on a cassette, which is a beautiful and simple way to leave your knowledge and legacy behind for family and friends. We had wonderful volunteers who would read to patients, play cards with them, and assist in their projects when necessary.

A former artist made delightful sketches of her cats; she had several which her family brought in one at a time for visits. Petting and playing with pets has been found to be so beneficial to healing and pain control, that a home for the elderly in my city now allows residents to keep pets. If you've always had pets, do your best to keep them with you at this time.

Friends, neighbors, or volunteers are often happy to assist in exercising or caring for your pet.

You might choose to spend more time with a favorite hobby: gardening, quilting, stamp collecting, photography; or start a new one you've never had time for.   When cancer interrupted one of our young patient's quest for an education, he continued his studies at home and obtained his college degree.   I read about a thirty-seven year old woman who got her real estate agent's license while living in a Hospice, and with the help of her husband sold two houses before she died.   On the lighter side, one man had always wanted to ride in a helicopter and with the help of a local broadcasting company he was granted his wish. 1

I saw the glow of pride and pleasure on the faces of those terminally ill persons who fulfilled their goals. Even if death interrupted their completion, they seemed satisfied that they had used their last days in the best way they could think of.

Some people may shake their heads and ask," Why bother?" when they see such ambitions in the dying person. They are looking at the dying process from the outside and can't understand that when you are in that place of life's time limit, you know that nothing we learn or experience at any time is wasted.   When you come to the point of serious contemplation about your life, and the meaning of all life, you will find that deep place of wisdom inside yourself that tells you nothing we create of value or beauty disappears completely.

We now have the shining example of Kenneth B. Schwartz who accomplished his most memorable work during the brief period of his terminal illness. Suffering with metastatic lung cancer at the age of forty, he wrote an article published in the Boston Globe Magazine, telling about his hospital experiences. ". . .the ordeal has been punctuated by moments of exquisite compassion. . . I've been touched by the smallest kind gestures - a squeeze of my hand, a gentle touch, a reassuring word. In some ways these quiet acts of humanity have felt more healing than the high dose of radiation and chemotherapy that hold the hope of a cure."

Before he died he founded a non-profit organization called the "Kenneth B. Schwartz Center" to promote this kind of compassionate caregiving. It is housed at the Massachusetts General Hospital, and is dedicated to strengthening the relationship between patients and caregivers through education, training and support; advocacy and policy development; and research. [2]

Additional Reading

Lon G. Nungesser, "Notes on Living Until We Say Goodbye", St. Martins Press, NY 1988.

Robert L. Veninga, "A Gift of Hope: How We Survive our Tragedies", Ballantine Books, NY 1985.

Dr. Elizabeth Kubler Ross, "To Live Until We Say Goodbye", Prentice Hall, NJ, 1978.

Norman Cousins, "Anatomy of an Illness as Perceived by the Patient: Reflections of Healing and Regeneration", G. K. Hall, Boston, 1980.

George Shehan, "Going the Distance", Villard Books, NY, 1996.

Chapter III
How to Tell Others

At this point you may be asking yourself something like, "How can I think about doing anything good when I'm worried about my spouse managing the house alone? Who's going to take care of my children, my pet? Who's going to take care of me if I get much weaker? How can I afford medication?"

It's becoming clear that you need help solving these and other problems, and one or two health partners will not be able to handle it. You need the help of all the people who care about you. If you haven't already done so, it's time to enlist the aid of your family and friends.

Bearing up under the diagnoses and worsening of disease all by yourself intensifies your sense of being singled out, isolated, alone with a terrible secret. One of the greatest fears in the dying process is being shunned and abandoned. The need to gather a caring group of supporters around you is a good reason to tell your family and friends about your illness. Why then, do some of us fear to include our loved ones in our difficult experience?

One of the reasons we fear telling people about a serious illness, is that it identifies us as 'the sick one' and makes people act differently toward us. It also confirms that identity for us, and we start to think of ourselves as 'the sick one'.

SELF-CONDEMNATION

Perhaps you've been blaming yourself for what is happening to your body, and you imagine others pointing fingers at you with, "You shouldn't have done that." Unless your disease is something that was imbedded in your genes when you were born, it is possible that you unwittingly contributed to contracting or exacerbating your illness. Guilty feelings plague us when we view all our yesterday's actions in the light of today's knowledge.

Only psychotic people deliberately set out to harm their bodies. The rest of us seek to enjoy the pleasure of some good, or find a pleasant method of lifting our spirits or relieving the tedium and pressures of daily life. Then we find out, "what felt good for us was bad for us", whether it was smoking, drinking, drugs, overeating, or sex (not always safe). Maybe we wanted to make more money, have more power and control over our life, get more of the good things available, so we ruined our health with overwork, ignoring our body, no relaxation, self-inflicted stress, lack of exercise or recreation.

Just about everyone you know takes part in some of the above. Those who point fingers at you show a lack of understanding of the frailty of human nature. If you can't weed fault finders out of your company, ignore them. Start now to put blame aside and accept human beings for the frequently misguided creatures that we are.

Another reason why it's hard to admit you have an incurable illness is that some people may actually shun you and start making excuses for not being with you, especially if your disease is considered contagious. This is what made suffering with Hanson's disease, formerly called Leprosy, so heartbreaking. And the new Human Immunodeficiency Virus, with its threat of contagion, labels its victims with a perceived stigma of being immoral and socially unacceptable.

Whether you have such a stigmatized illness or not, you don't have to tell everybody, especially your co-workers or boss if you'd risk losing your job. You don't have to tell the guys at the racket club, or the girls in your aerobics class, because they might look at you as a source of contagion. Don't tell Aunt Sophie if you know she won't understand, or Grandma and Grandpa if you're afraid it would be too distressing for them. You can tell your clergyman the news, but ask him to keep it confidential if you're not ready to share it with your church community. All of these people will find out sooner or later, but if you suspect they won't support you, later is better.

TELLING OUR LOVED ONES

But why is it hard to reveal your illness to those closest to you, those you live with and interact with daily? All of the above reasons, plus wishing to spare them pain and trouble. The problem is, you're probably already causing them distress, especially if you've been trying to hide your illness for a long time.

You've been through a great deal of physical and emotional trauma, and without realizing it you are now relating to others differently. You've begun grieving over the future loss of the good things you have in your life, and you may already be anticipating the pain of parting with all your loved ones. Grief of this scope has made you think and act differently, though you may not be aware of it.

* * *

One of the common reactions to facing a life-threatening illness is anger. It's natural to have angry feelings about this interruption in your plans and ambitions, about your failing health with the restrictions it places on your activity, perhaps even the loss of your job. When you look in the mirror, you may discover changes in your appearance and be sad or angry about losing your former physical attractiveness, and all those attributes you used to take for granted.

Maybe your angry feelings have already surfaced and you've lashed out at your doctor for not curing you, or at health professionals for not making you feel better. You may have snapped at friends or family without meaning to. Your angry feelings may sometimes be directed at an inanimate object that got in your way, or at no one, and nothing in particular. You may simply feel irritable and short tempered and don't know why, but the feelings make you act differently than you did before.

* * *

You may notice subtle differences in your interactions with family members and friends. There may be a stiffness or nervousness about their demeanor, and conversation doesn't flow as easily as it used to. That's because you look like the same person, but inwardly everyone senses a change, and change makes us uneasy. Only you can put an end to this uneasiness before it gets any worse, and it will. Because you are the central focus of the changes taking place, take charge of the situation and begin the dialogue which will open the way for honest expression of thoughts and feelings.

You can break it to them gradually by talking about your failing health, your visit to the doctor, and finally his diagnosis of your illness. Be sure and call the actual illness by name so that no one, not even yourself, can skirt around the truth. Once you've told them, be prepared for the flood of emotions and the questions. Answer them honestly and simply. Now is not the time for details about tests, treatments, or results. If they want to know all that, they will ask.

There, you've told them, and for the rest of your days you can talk about your disease openly in your household. You will find this is a great relief. You also have the attention and compassion of those you will need to help you travel the difficult road of severe illness. It's still not going to be easy for any of you, but life was seldom easy before. Together you will be able to face the new problems your illness has brought with it.

ALTERED THOUGHTS AND FEELINGS

Just the fact that everyone now knows that you have a serious illness has shaken those secure feelings that a business-as-usual existence carries with it. You may have been trying hard to keep everyone's routine flowing normally. It's wise to make as few changes as possible, but there is an unavoidable disruption of routine thought patterns, and you may have been forced to make some changes in the daily living routine.

Perhaps your role was formerly the breadwinner, caregiver, comforter, housekeeper, or authority figure and now you are the one that will need taking care of. Everyone must adjust their way of relating to you which may sound simple but is psychologically very difficult.

* * *

Emotional disturbances have arisen because your loved ones may be anticipating losing your presence among them and have already started to grieve. An instinctive protective device in our human nature can cause us to start withdrawing emotionally and physically from our dying loved ones to eliminate the pain of separation at the end.

I witnessed such a withdrawal in a children's hospital in which a young boy was losing a battle with leukemia. His parents began to distance themselves from him by visiting him less frequently. When they did visit, they no longer held and cuddled him as they had formerly. The hospital staff did their best to shower the child with attention and affection to ward off the sense of loneliness and feelings of abandonment his parents were inflicting on him. Counseling gradually helped the parents understand their feelings and change their withdrawal patterns so that at the end they were there for their child.

The tactic of withdrawal does not work successfully because the pain of loss at the end remains, and it is accompanied by guilt and remorse over lost opportunities to support the loved one during life.

* * *

You can expect still another problem to arise. Our societal conditioning in this country prompts us to fear and avoid death. The possibility of your dying highlights the fragility of life and reminds those around you that someday they, too, will die. Death is rarely spoken of honestly in our society and bringing up the subject is considered poor taste. Even the most devoted spouse, parent, child, or friend can feel uneasy and become tongue-tied when the specter of death is present. They may want to talk with you about their feelings but feel too awkward and unsure. Some friends may start avoiding you for that very reason.

As we discussed above, an especially difficult interaction arises if your family and friends feel you were in some way responsible for your illness. One of them may disagree about your choice of treatments, or your rejection of treatments. Those who work with the dying occasionally witness these painful rifts between the terminally ill individual and their family.

Sometimes the divisions are between various family members when they disagree over who is at fault, who should have prevented this, or how treatment should have proceeded. There is frequently one relative making demands for tests and treatments of doubtful benefit to the patient. I witnessed one death in the hospice which was made much more difficult because two opposing factions of relatives refused to speak to each other. Working through these angry feelings can sometimes be facilitated by a social worker, psychologist, therapist, or pastoral care minister, but at other times nothing has been able to help.

* * *

There are ways to heal rifts in personal re-lationships right at the beginning of your illness, and insure that you will never have to suffer the painful death and dying scenes described above. You can put an end to uneasy feelings that arise as soon as you perceive them, and get everyone back to feeling comfortable with each other. It requires that everyone begin thinking and speaking honestly about the kinds of thoughts and feelings they've been having.

If you and your loved ones have always shared your thoughts and feelings with each other without hedging on the truth, without burying disagreeable facts, and without the subterfuge of disguising certain feelings, you have a good start on the open communication you will need to get through this. As difficult as it seems at times to tell all, and to hear all the truth, it is the best possible way for you and your loved ones to work through your illness and dying. Those who have taken the courageous path of absolute openness and honesty find out at the end that it was the most painless way after all.

ACHIEVING OPEN COMMUNICATION

If you find that open communication is a problem, you may want to give your loved ones this manual and let them read the above paragraphs of this chapter. Then, either individually or as a group, ask them to think about and express at least one aspect of their changing feelings. Be prepared for tears and sadness because there's going to be buried pain rising to the surface.

If your family members talk freely about their feelings it will be easy. If such openness is not common it might be easier to have everyone start by writing down thoughts and feelings ahead of time. Others may hesitate to mention your illness because of the pain it may cause you, so it's best for you to open the dialogue first.

* * *

Use "I" messages when talking about sensitive subjects. For instance open with the words, "I've been thinking a lot about my sickness and I feel very sad about having to leave all of you if I die." Or, "I know I've been crabby lately, it's nothing you've done, I'm just so angry about having this illness."

Avoid "you" messages that focus on what you want others to do, say, or feel because they tend to make others defensive. The wrong opening would be something like, "You've been acting as if something is bothering you lately." Or, "You seem to resent the fact that I can't do the housework anymore."

Listen carefully to every person's response. Talk about the concerns they voice and the feelings they show. You may want to repeat what is said in your own words to make sure you understand it correctly. For instance, "I hear you saying that you haven't talked about my illness because you were afraid it would hurt me." Be prepared to clarify misunderstandings by answering questions and by asking questions.

Disagreements can occur which aren't settled easily. Impatience and anger may erupt with everyone talking and nobody listening. If this should happen call a halt to the discussion, ask everyone to relax, and then follow the 'Bridge to Solve Problems' you will find at the end of this chapter. If, after a few attempts at this, one or two members take offense or will not agree on a solution, let it go. At least you have the satisfaction of doing your best to solve the problem.

The intensity of this kind of dialogue is tiring and you probably won't be able to discuss everything in one session. Setting specific dates and times for other discussions will insure that everything gets talked out. For example, plan ahead by saying, "Let's talk about this again after dinner tomorrow", or, "at three o'clock on Sunday." Don't put off the next discussion for more than a day or two.

After the first session, informal conversations about subjects may flow more easily and there may be an easing of tension in your relationships. But don't stop now. The first session opens the way for more thoughts and feelings which need to be brought into the open. After many sessions you will probably begin to communicate honestly and openly at all times which is the goal to be achieved. Your love and understanding of each other will grow into a bond which can withstand any separation, even that of death.

The most delicate communication is required between you and your spouse or significant loved one. Emotions will run high and sometimes make speech impossible. No matter how busy both of you are, it's imperative to spend at least fifteen minutes, more if possible, alone together every day. Your remaining days together may be limited and you need to speak about that truthfully, but in the most tender way possible. If having sex will be a problem at sometime in your illness, or if it is already, discuss ways to compensate for that. If you may be hospitalized, talk about how you will each manage without the other's companionship.   Instead of long term goals, make short term plans for doing things together.

Professionals who work in the field of death and dying call the above process "anticipatory grief work". It is a major factor in healing the third fear of dying which is separation from our loved ones. I witnessed many successful examples of pre-death grief work in which family members who were barely speaking to each other became reconciled. Still others in which families who were already communicating their feelings well, bonded even more closely with each other and with their dying loved one. At the end there was sadness, or course, but also an aura of content in knowing that all misunderstandings had been healed, and all the final goodbyes had been spoken.

Elton John and Bernie Taupin wrote "The Last Song" in memory of a young man dying of AIDS. In poetic form, it gives us a beautiful example of this kind of pre-death grief work. In one verse the young man describes a reconciliation with his estranged father. He talks about the unspoken words that were haunting him and coming between them.   Sharing these truths sets him free. 3

Additional Reading

Martin Shepard, "Someone You Love is Dying", Harmony Books, NY, 1975.

Herbert & Kay Kramer, "Conversations at Midnight", Wm. Morrow & Co., NY, 1993.

Mary Pipher, "Another Country: Exploring the Emotional Terrain of our Elders, Riverhead Books, 1999.

A Bridge to Solve Problems

Rules: Be honest.
Keep responses to one or two sentences.
Don't interrupt while someone else is speaking.
Stick to the subject in question.
No name calling.

Step 1. One at a time, each person tells what they want.
Step 2. Each person has a turn telling what they heard the others say.
Step 3. One at a time, each person tells how they feel.
Step 4. Each person has a turn telling what they heard the others say about their feelings.
Step 5. Between all of you come up with three ideas or solutions.
Step 6. Set a time limit for discussing them, then decide on the best solution.

Chapter IV
Legal Loose Ends

It takes time to incorporate the truth of your failing health into your conscious and subconscious mind and meanwhile you must keep forcing yourself to go about your business. During these early stages you may start going through your insurance policies, find an attorney to set up your will, start working out plans to sell the house, give up your apartment and move in with someone else, or set up trust funds for your children.

There are a number of legal documents you may want to prepare at this time, and sometimes the distraction of doing them seems like a welcome relief. Also, taking care of this practical business gives you the assurance that you still have some control over your life.

If you've been handling your own finances up till now it's a good idea to set up a Power of Attorney and have it registered where you bank. This appointed person will be able to sign your checks, pay your bills, and handle your other financial transactions if you become unable to do so. Your health partner may be willing to take on this task. If not, a friend or relative who lives in your locality and has some knowledge of finances would be a good choice.

A legal form for this purpose is available at office supply stores and hospital admitting offices, or your attorney can prepare the document for you. Your bank will keep a copy of this document and ask you and your appointee to sign their authorization forms. This Power of Attorney appointment is only honored while you are alive and it becomes invalid at your death when all your financial holdings revert to your estate. Regulations may vary in different states. Your attorney or bank adviser will have that information.

AUTHORIZATION TO RELEASE MEDICAL INFORMATION

Talk to your physician about the forms he needs to release the information from your medical chart to someone other than a family member, your health partner for instance. This will be necessary if you become unable to review your chart and make your own decisions. Try to get downsized copies of the pertinent records in your care to carry with you if you travel. In an emergency it will avoid wasting time while strange physicians research your records and treatments.

A LIVING WILL

This is a good time to think about a Durable Power of Attorney, or the more common Power of Attorney for Health Care, or a Living Will. When signed and witnessed properly it is legal documentation that specifies what life-sustaining measures you may want or not want if you are not conscious or otherwise unable to express your wishes. The common ones are Cardiopulmonary Resuscitation, tube feedings, mechanical ventilation, and IV fluids, but there are others. If you're not sure, you may want to consult with someone in the health care field as to all the types of life-sustaining measures that can be used, when they are a good idea, and when they are not. Social workers at your hospital or hospice are available to assist you with this form.

A Living Will is a simple one-page statement that you do not want to be revived by heroic measures if you cannot be restored to viable functioning, and are unable to communicate this at the time. It must be signed in the presence of two witnesses.

POWER OF ATTORNEY FOR HEALTH CARE

A Power of Attorney for Health Care states in more detail what you desire in such a case, and appoints persons who have the authority to speak for you when you are not able. This document contains a blank section in which you may write additional directives that are not contained in the printed text. Your doctor may point out some of the specific instructions you can add for example: I want to be given antibiotics if I develop an infection; if I am unable to move I want to receive passive range of motion exercises to prevent muscle contractures; or, I want to be turned and massaged regularly to prevent bed sores. If you have these papers prepared by your attorney be sure to inform him of your special requests so they can be added.

For this document you choose a health care Power of Attorney and an alternate health care Power of Attorney. The term 'attorney' does not mean that these persons are members of the legal profession, and they can be chosen from among your relatives or friends. Read through the document with them explaining fully what you would like done in specific cases so they clearly understand your intentions.

A copy of this should be with your doctor and in your medical chart if you are in the hospital or a health care facility. Also, a copy each for your health care attorneys, and the original stays with you. Some states have a five-year limit on the validity of these documents, after which time they must be redone.

After my husband recovered from a heart attack, we talked over, and decided on our preferences for end of life choices. We obtained preprinted forms and the instructions accompanying them from our State Health Department (address and phone number in the Government listings of your phone book) and had no difficulty completing them. We reviewed our wishes with those we had chosen to be our health care attorneys, and signed them in the presence of two witnesses (not our appointed health care attorneys). Copies of them are now in our doctors' charts.

* * *

A recent nation-wide survey of 2,162 patients diagnosed with six months or less to live, revealed that only 23% had discussed their end-of-life preferences for CPR with their physicians. These were also the patients who had made out the health care documents described above. The others left these decisions to their physician, or the hospital personnel on duty at the time of death. As a result, some were resuscitated and put on long-term mechanical ventilation, and some were allowed to die naturally. If you desire to have such life support systems used or not, it's important to make your wishes known in a legal document, and in discussion with your doctor.

YOUR LAST WILL AND TESTAMENT

Now is a good time to make out your Last Will and Testament, but it isn't an easy task.   Whether we are eighteen or eighty we've grown fond of at least a few of our possessions and it's difficult to think about parting with them.

When college friends, Donna and Marcie set up housekeeping as roommates, they combined their furniture and household equipment, and added to it as the years went by. When Donna drowned in a freak accident, her family came a few days after the funeral and carried off all her personal belongings: clothes; accessories; photographs; plants; wall hangings; all of the furniture and household equipment they thought was hers, including some of the jointly owned pieces.

Marcie protested, but found she had no written proof of ownership, and no legal recourse to prevent Donna's parents from taking anything they wanted. Marcie's grief at losing Donna was increased by the loss of all the shared personal mementos of their friendship, plus many of the furnishings she needed. This loss could have been prevented if they had each prepared simple wills designating their beneficiaries.

The time of crisis that finds us coping with a serious illness may seem like the worst time to make our Last Will and Testament because we already have so many problems pressing down on us. The truth is, there is never a good time to plan for the disbursement of our belongings.

While we are healthy and think of ourselves as having many years ahead, listing our property and deciding who gets what is the farthest thing from our minds. You may realize that now, during this illness, you need to get the job done, but your heart resists making the necessary decisions and legal documents which will make your wishes clear and binding.

A strategy that has helped others in making a Will is looking at this dispersal as the giving of good gifts to the loved ones you must leave behind. We pass on to them the fruits of our labors and the treasured mementoes which are part of our lives. We are giving them tangible memories of ourselves.

* * *

If you have already made your Will, the following ideas may prompt you to make some additions or changes. If you haven't, the following tips will help you get started. Remember, working on this difficult task now will make the transition smoother for those you love, and having a Will will minimize costs of settling your estate and generally minimize estate taxes. It may be the case that it will help to insure your family's financial stability after you are gone.

In most states the progression of inheritance without a Will is as follows (some states may have differing progression): surviving spouse inherits all; surviving spouse inherits as much as the first $150,000 plus half the balance, before those children who are yours only, but not your spouse's inherit; if no spouse, children get equal shares; if there are no living children, grandchildren get equal shares; next in order follow great grandchildren; parents; brothers and sisters; nephews and nieces; grand nephews and nieces; great grandnephews and nieces; grandparents; uncles and aunts; first cousins; first cousins once removed; first cousins twice removed; first cousins thrice removed. You can see that without a Will all your possessions could go to someone you didn't intend, perhaps someone you never knew existed.

Before you contact an attorney to make out the legal document, it's a good idea to think ahead and jot down a list of the assets you own, then make out a plan of financial and property disbursements. All this preparation gets to be a lot of work when you are under the strain of a serious illness and are already feeling poorly. Can your health partner take on another task for you? If not, you need to choose one trusted friend or relative to act as Executor/Executrix of your Will, and this person can help you in the planning stage if necessary. In the hospice, volunteers or social workers would sometimes help in listing possessions and benefactors, but were never allowed to make decisions for the clients or be included in the Will.

If you're married it is most likely that you'll want your surviving spouse to receive all your possessions, and you may even choose your spouse to be your Executor. In some states a surviving spouse automatically inherits all properties unless specific provisions are made in a Will. It is still wise for each spouse to make an individual Will because of the possibility of the unexpected death of both of you. If you have minor children, be sure to appoint a guardian for them, in case this should happen. Otherwise a court of law will have to appoint a guardian for them.

If you have many blood relatives, particularly a number of children, you may not want to leave equal portions of your estate to each one. You may decide that some are in greater need of, or would value certain properties, more than others. There may be a caregiver or other close friend you want to remember in your Will. You may also have dedicated yourself to certain charitable works and wish to bequeath part of your estate to a charitable organization. These are your tangible goods and you have the right to disburse them as you wish.

The best way to avoid hurt feelings or downright anger over your decisions is to explain your intentions and your reasons to each person involved, either as a group or individually. Listening to their comments carefully and answering their questions will help to facilitate understanding. This communication may cause you to rethink some decisions and change your plan. If not, you are ready to prepare the final papers.

* * *

A legal document for a Will involving a variety of assets and a number of relatives and benefactors is usually best handled by an attorney. If you don't already have one you may want to discuss your needs with several and consider their fees before choosing one. If your possessions and your benefactors or relatives are few, you may choose to make your own Will. Last Will and Testament forms can be purchased at office supply stores, and Will preparation kits are advertised in the newspaper and magazines. A Last Will and Testament Preparation Kit contains all the information needed to plan and prepare a simple Will with fill-in-the-blank forms for a variety of situations. They are easy to use and when properly signed and witnessed are legally binding. Some states require that you sign before two witnesses, and some states require three. They do not have to be notarized.

After your Will is completed and signed, the attorney, if you have one will keep a copy, you will keep the original, perhaps in a safe deposit box, and your Executor may keep a copy or at least be aware of where you keep the original. It's a good idea to keep all of your important papers together and inform your Executor where they will be kept.

THE LETTER OF INSTRUCTION

A Letter of Instruction is sometimes prepared along with a Will although it is not a legally binding document. It can contain those wishes that cannot be included in your Will, such as funeral and burial arrangements. Prepaid funerals are becoming more common and if you do this, the name of the funeral parlor, a brief description of your arrangements and the amount paid should be listed here. Today's funeral directors are trained to help you fill out forms to obtain Social Security benefits, file insurance claims, and secure survivor's pension benefits so if you are prearranging your funeral, discuss these forms as well.

If you have already made plans to die in your own home, or are considering the possibility, inform your director at this time. He will explain the procedure of transporting your body from home to his establishment. Most funeral homes now have twenty-four hour transportation services available for this purpose.

In your letter of instruction you may also include detailed wishes of a specific outfit of clothing or jewelry you want used, what type of religious service, if any, including the name of the church, and any particular prayers or songs you prefer. If you have chosen a cemetery and paid for a plot or a place in a mausoleum, include that information as well.

If you wish to donate your body to a Medical College, state with whom such arrangement was made. Make sure your caregivers know about this at the time of your death. You must have the donation forms on file with the school ahead of time. Some schools have age at death requirements and will not accept the very elderly and infirm. Most will not take amputees. Make sure your body will meet their specifications.

State your intention to donate body organs in this letter of instruction, but make sure caregivers know about this at time of death. Eye corneas and tissues can be used from almost anyone, but only the young and healthy can donate other body parts.

The National Funeral Directors Association recommends specific information be included in the Letter of Instruction. I have printed their suggested format at the end of this chapter.

SEPARATE WRITING IDENTIFYING BEQUEST OF TANGIBLE PROPERTY

In a letter of instruction you can tell how to disperse personal property that is not listed in a will such as family photos, plants, pets, china, silverware, crystal, jewelry, furniture, and so forth, but if you want these bequests to be legally binding you must prepare a "Separate Writing Identifying Bequest of Tangible Property", and state the existence of this "List" in your Will. The list must be in your handwriting or signed by you, and people mentioned as benefactors in it must be clearly identified, for example: my niece, Betty Jones, the Fostoria crystal stemware.

* * *

Division of these personal effects is often more difficult than estate items such as stocks, bonds, and property, because of the feelings of attachment family members have toward them. A study done by the University of Minnesota revealed major, long-lasting conflicts between family members over such items. Their publication entitled "Who Gets Grandma's Pie Plate? Transferring Non-titled Property," explains the differences in perceptions of fairness involved in the division of such personal goods.   I have included instructions for obtaining copies of their suggestions at the end of this chapter.

The study recommends holding meetings with the family members who will receive your personal belongings. You can have the pleasure of giving them items as gifts and telling about the memories connected with them.   You can also hear the stories of family members who would like certain items because of special memories they have of them.

You may not be ready to part with these things as yet, in fact you may likely still be using some of them, so carefully record all items to be given away, to whom they were given, and a short description of the memory connected with them. Be sure to date this record and have all family members present, as well as yourself, sign it so that no mistakes will be made at distribution time.

My mother-in-law accumulated a houseful of treasures in her ninety-eight years, and distribution of them was a lengthy process. It seemed impossible to have family discussions about all of them so she used the "masking tape" technique. She kept a roll of masking tape handy and when family members visited she instructed them to tape their name on the bottom of things they would like to inherit. At first everyone felt shy about this premature claiming of her goods, but after her repeated urgings they began to lay claim to what they really wanted. Masking tape can get smudged, torn, or be removed so she eventually had a friend record the items and the person who wanted them in a ledger.

* * *

While you are going through the emotional adjustments of a life-threatening illness, all of these preparations and legal matters can begin to seem overwhelming. Take care of the vital arrangements now and postpone others for a later date. Tackle it in small stages and get as many caregivers and family members to assist as you can. In the end it is your loved ones who will benefit from your having tied up all these loose ends. Your reward will be the immense feeling of relief and satisfaction in knowing that all these matters are taken care of.

Items to be included in your Letter of Instruction

Full name
Maiden name
Date and place of birth
Names and birthplaces of parents,
      if living address and phone number
Social Security number
Date and place of marriage
Name and address of spouse
Names and addresses of previous spouses
Names, addresses, and phone numbers of brothers,
      sisters, dependents or children
Other relatives to be contacted
Friends, employers, colleagues to be contacted
Religious affiliation, name and address of church
Membership in professional and fraternal organizations
Highschools/colleges attended, including place and
      dates
Which newspapers/publications should run an obituary
Part of the body to be donated to medical science
Funeral director, Funeral Home, amount prepaid
Instructions for visitation
Clergy person or others to preside over service,
      deliver eulogy or readings
Type of service

Special instructions for hymns, prayers, readings
Donations to be made in your honor
Names, addresses, and phone numbers of casket
      bearers
Location of Will along with name, address, and phone
      numbers of attorney and/or executor
Location of safety deposit box, if any, with name and
      address of bank where located
Location and account numbers of checking and savings
      accounts
Location of checkbooks, passbooks, and other
      certificates
Location, name, and number for charge accounts and
      credit cards
Location of insurance policies, ownership title to cars
      and other property

If you are a veteran you may also want to include:

Date and place of enlistment
Rank and service number
Organization or outfit
Commendations received
Location of discharge papers
Flag desired to drape casket

How to obtain the publication "It's Only Grandma's Pie Plate, Disbursement of Personal Property" contact:

Minnesota University Extension Service
Distribution Center, 20 Coffey Hall
1420 Eckles Ave.
St. Paul, Minnesota 55108
(612)625-8173 or (612)625-2722

Additional Reading:

Earl A. Grollman, "Concerning Death: A Practical Guide for the Living", Beacon Press, Boston, 1974.

Gregory W. Young, "The High Cost of Dying: a Guide to Funeral Planning", Prometheus Books, N.Y. 1994

John C. Howell, "How to Write Your Own Will", Liberty Publishing Co., Maryland, 1985

Getting Comfortable

Those who work with the terminally ill have discovered that people are more afraid of the process of dying than of the event of death itself. However, it's not the horrible experience that many imagine it to be. When it becomes clear that nothing more can be done to effect a cure, compassionate care never ceases. The right doctors and supportive staff will see to it that your highest quality of life is maintained throughout the process. Both you and your family can take comfort in knowing that there is never a time in terminal illness in which nothing more can be done.

Our greatest fear is that it's going to hurt a lot, and for a long time. Pain at the present moment, and fear of more pain in the future, is the most debilitating factor in the lives of those with incurable illnesses. Maybe you've been in pain while fighting this illness, especially during your hospital stays undergoing treatments.   Erase those images from your mind because during the time you have left you don't have to suffer.

Your pain has served to alert you to a bodily malfunction that needed attention.   Now that your problem has been reported and is being looked after pain is no longer needed.   Insist that your physician and caregivers use every means at their disposal to eliminate it.

Traditional medical practice is based on the approach of limiting pain medication to no more than is absolutely necessary. In practice it means that patients must wait to start hurting before they ask for pain medication. Then they must wait ten minutes to forty-five minutes, depending on the type of medication, for it to take effect and relieve them of their pain. Sometimes this is necessary during an acute illness when 'masking the pain' disguises the nature and severity of the problem. Most often it is the rule of medical practice because it is thought to be the best way to manage pain. This method is responsible for much suffering among the incurably ill.

GOOD PAIN CONTROL

Hospice physicians, their trained staff, and supporting therapists involved in working with patients who endure chronic pain as the result of an incurable disease, believe that patients should not suffer at all. To achieve good pain control they give medication in advance, before the pain begins, and then at regular intervals without waiting for sensations of pain to break through. The aim is to erase the memory of suffering and eliminate the fear of pain in the future.

When suffering patients enter a hospice care system they are given a maximum amount of medication to halt discomfort immediately. The dose is then adjusted gradually until the minimum amount necessary to maintain good pain control is reached. The aim is to control the pain and other symptoms without inducing dizziness or drowsiness. This is sometimes a difficult balance, but advanced pain management techniques have about a 90% success rate. These techniques include not only a variety of medications, but also long-term nerve blocks, radiation to shrink tumors and relieve pressure on surrounding tissues, and electrical units designed to interrupt nerve impulses.

Drowsiness is common during the first few days of your pain control therapy, because pain has kept you from getting sufficient rest. When you have gotten all the sleep you need, and your pain medication is properly adjusted, you will be clear headed and remain awake.

In about ten per cent of cases, even with the best of physicians and techniques, there are some types of pain that cannot be eliminated without diminishing the alertness and mental capacity of the patient. Most patients and their loved ones find this is preferable to unrelieved pain. Also, certain types of diseases involve nerve tissue of the brain and spinal cord, which causes severe mental agitation or continual, terrifying hallucinations. Barbiturates can be used to eliminate these, but they also completely sedate the patient. Compassionate care and consideration for family members sometimes require that this be done.

During this process of adjusting your medication, you may be asked to describe any breakthrough pain with questions such as: "is it sharp, stabbing, burning, aching, throbbing, grinding, tingling, itching?" You may also be asked how severe the pain is on a scale of one to ten, with one being no pain and ten being the worst pain you can imagine. If you've been hospitalized during your illness you're probably already familiar with the routine.

For your added comfort and to protect your skin integrity, pain injections are avoided whenever possible. Most pain medications are available in tablet, capsule or liquid form. If nausea, vomiting, or inability to swallow make this method impossible, many medications can be administered in the form of suppositories, or a skin patch. A patch looks like a large 3x3 inch bandaid, covered with a specialized form of pain medication that is absorbed through your skin. It is usually applied on the upper torso and kept intact for several days.

* * *

If your present physician is not keeping your pain under control in the manner described above, don't hesitate to find one that will. You cannot achieve quality of life for your remaining days until you are pain-free. Many people are surprised to find out how much more energy they have when their pain is gone.

RESISTANCE TO PAIN MEDICATION

You may feel uneasy about the possible damage done to your body by taking strong and unnatural substances for pain. This is a valid fear. Ask your doctor to explain the harm done to your body by the stress of unremitting pain vs. the side effects of the medication, so you can make an informed decision. It's important that you understand all the aspects of your care, and make your wishes known to your doctor and caregivers.

Controlling pain so that we can live to our fullest capacity seems to be a logical decision, yet some people feel that their self-worth is threatened by taking large amounts of pain medication. While growing up, many of us have absorbed a litany of "should's and shouldn't's" with regard to pain and suffering:

- I shouldn't let my pain show, it's a sign of weakness.
- I should suffer bravely to become a man/woman.
- I should endure pain, it builds character.
- I should accept my pain, it's God's will.
- I should suffer to make up for being a bad person.
- I should suffer to become a better person.
- I shouldn't take medication to stop pain, it's cowardly.
- I shouldn't take medicine for pain, because I won't be able to stop.
- I should avoid narcotic medications so I don't become a drug addict.
- I shouldn't take narcotics for pain because my friends and family will think I'm a drug addict.

Have you unconsciously absorbed any of these statements into your belief system? If you have been resisting your doctor's prescription for pain control, or feel guilty or uneasy when you take the medication, one of these moral injunctions may be the culprit. Even if you can't identify with a particular statement, talk to your doctor about your feelings. He may be able to allay your fears, or he may refer you to a counselor, psychologist, pastoral care minister, or a support group.

If your loved ones criticize you, or warn you about the danger of becoming a drug addict, ask your doctor to explain the facts to them. Studies show that 98% of patients whose cause of chronic pain is cured, are willingly and successfully able to wean themselves from pain medication. For those who are approaching death, the fear of drug addiction is irrelevant.

TREATING SYMPTOMS

As important as good pain control, is relieving any disagreeable symptoms you may have. They will differ in severity and range from any of the following and more: nausea, vomiting, shortness of breath, dizziness, rashes, difficulty swallowing, indigestion, pressure sores, headaches, constipation, diarrhea, incontinence, muscle cramps, dry mouth, and fever. Quality care requires that each symptom be treated as a separate disease and brought under control.

Be diligent in keeping track of all such symptoms, the time of day they occur, how severe they are, what, if any, activity brings them on. Then take the prescribed medication noting any disagreeable side effects, and follow the prescribed treatments or procedures faithfully, noting how well they work or don't work.

It's helpful to keep a notebook handy to jot down the above information as it occurs. If you prefer you can make a chart with your symptoms in one column, when they occur in the next column, the medication and it's side effects in the next column, and the treatment and it's effectiveness in another.

If all this sounds like a lot of work, it is. Whether you are living alone and have been taking care of yourself, are with your spouse, or are dwelling in the midst of a family, it's time to start thinking about getting some help.   You have always made preparations for the big events in your life so it makes sense to plan for the changes that must take place in your lifestyle because of your failing health.

Additional Reading

Sandol Stoddard, "The Hospice Movement", Random House, N.Y., 1978.

U.S. Pharmacopeial, "Advice for the Patient: Drug Information in Lay Language", 7th Edition. U.S. Pharmacopeial Convention, Inc. 1987.

Sylvia Lack and Robert G. Twycross, "Oral Morphine: Information for Patients, Families, and Friends", England, 1995, Order from: Roxanne Laboratories, Inc., P.O. Box 16532 Columbus, Ohio 43216.

American Pain Society
4700 West Lake Ave.,
Glenview IL 60025
847-375-4700,   www.ampainsoc.org
E-mail: info@ampainsoc.org
Publishes "Pain Facilities Directory" listing over 500
pain treatment centers across the country.

American Chronic Pain Association
P. O. Box 850
Rocklin, CA 95677
916-632-0922,   www.theacpa.org
Offers educational material and peer support to help
combat, cope with, and/or live with chronic pain.
Referral to a support group near you.

Chapter VI
Gathering Support

In her writings about the Hospice Movement, Sandol Stoddard says that dying, like giving birth, requires a great deal of work, and we need caring people about us to help.4   If you prefer to remain in your own home how much of your care can your spouse or family manage?   If you are alone, is it possible to arrange for a relative, friend, or live-in home companion to stay with you?   Call your family members together to discuss your needs, because these are not only your personal problems but are situations that involve all of them. Remember you will only need their help during this time of your illness and some may be wanting to help but are not sure how.

At present you may be managing well with only a little assistance, but now is the time to plan ahead for periods when you will be too weak to accomplish much. If you are an independent person, it will be hard for you to ask your family and friends for help and tell them frankly what your needs are. Try writing them down ahead of time and rehearse what you will say aloud a few times.   Methods for honest communication discussed in Chapter Three will help you here.

In your list of needs be sure to include homemaking chores like meals, washing clothes, cleaning, shopping, and personal ones like bathing, toileting, toenail and hair care. If you are unable to drive you will need transportation for doctor visits and treatments. Discuss the amount of time each person has to help you, then divide up the tasks to suit each one's time and talents.

Keep a list of your helpers' tasks, and their phone numbers and addresses handy. Make sure other frequently used phone numbers and addresses are posted. Your helpers can then make necessary contacts without disturbing you.

It's much healthier for you to do for yourself all the activities of daily living that you can. Some may want to 'over-help' and allow you to do nothing, which will make you feel helpless. Tell them honestly, "This is something I can do for myself and I would rather do it myself."

Don't try to do more than one major task a day, and see how many daily activities you can eliminate or simplify. Use prepared foods, or make large casseroles or soups you can eat for several days. Cut down on dish washing by using paper plates and cups. Sign up for a "Meals on Wheels" service which will eliminate all food preparation on weekdays.

Can you afford a housecleaning service every week, or occasionally? You don't have to keep the house as spotless as you used to. Wear the same shirt or dress more than once to cut down on washing. Whatever work you can eliminate will lighten the load for yourself and for your helpers.

An answering machine is a wise investment to eliminate chasing to answer the phone, or talking to people who irritate you, or avoiding salespersons. Caring friends and relatives may call frequently to ask about any changes in your condition, or you may want to call and inform them. This can become very tiring. This type of communication may be another helpful task for your health partner, or for someone else who is unable to help in other ways.

Sometimes your helpers may need a little time to become competent in their tasks. Thank them first and tell them what a big help they are before you show them a better way to do something, or a way you would prefer something done. If you're having a bad day your helpers may feel sad or guilty because they can't make you feel better. Praise them lavishly for whatever they do, thank them constantly, and reassure them that they're doing a good job. Giving them praise and reassurance is important throughout your illness.

TELLING THE CHILDREN

If you have children or grandchildren, including them in the discussion of your needs gives them a sense of worth as important family members, and they can be given simple tasks. It will help them understand why the grownups can't give them as much attention as they are used to. They will learn a valuable lesson in seeing family members work together, and the spooky images they may have about people being sick or dying will be put to rest.

Children are happier having their sick mommy or daddy, sibling, or grandparent cared for at home, rather than out of sight at some mysterious place which everyone rushes off to but them. Children need to play, run, and laugh but can soon adapt to keeping quiet at certain times when a sick person needs sleep or rest.

Tell your child that you are very sick with (name the disease). Children feel more comfortable having a name for something. Even very young children can sense when there is tension in a household, or when someone is not feeling well. They may begin wondering if they've done something wrong. Reassure them as often as necessary that the difficulty is not their fault. Share your feelings with them and let them know that all kinds of feelings, even crying, are okay.

If you must enter a medical facility for treatments, pain or symptom control, tell your children ahead of time. Explain the reason why you must leave, and who will be taking care of them while you're gone. If you're not sure when you'll be back, be truthful about that. They'd be happier in their own home, but if they must go to Grandma's or Aunt Josephine's for care, explain that to them well ahead of time.

Don't send children away simply because you are getting sicker and might die soon. A child who has seen a parent, sibling, or grandparent die in their own home, surrounded by the peace and love of caring family members, won't be afraid of dying.

* * *

Children under the age of eight normally haven't absorbed our culture's death taboos, and can accept dying as a natural occurrence. My older sister was in an accident on the way home from school when I was five years old. My grandmother sat me down on her front steps in the care of neighbors while she rushed to the scene, which was only a block and a half away. Curious, I watched the growing crowd down on the next corner. After some time a neighbor came back, put her arm around me and said, "Your sister has gone to heaven to play with the angels." I remember feeling instantly happy, and envious too. I wanted to go with her. I never knew that neighbor's name, but I've often wanted to tell her it was a wonderful way to tell me about my sister's death. Her words have stayed with me all my life.

That same day a different adult asked me, "Aren't you going to cry? Your sister's dead." That surprised me. Why would I want to cry on such an exciting occasion? At that age I was unable to project into the future what the consequences of losing my only sister would be.

My sister's death taught me another valuable lesson. In those days Visitation Rites were held in the home, and my sister's body was to be laid out in our parlor. To prepare me, my grandmother explained that Geri had indeed gone to heaven but her body was badly hurt and she had to leave it behind. "It's going to look like her, but it's just and empty shell. She won't really be here." When the white casket surrounded by flowers was set up I pulled a chair over and climbed up to get a better look. It looked like Geri, only different. More like one of the painted statues in church. I touched her. Cold and hard like a statue. Grandma was right. This was just an empty shell. From that day to this I have never felt any repulsion in the presence of a dead body.

DYING AT HOME

The desire to protect the children, and even themselves, sometimes causes relatives to ship their dying loved one to a hospital when death is imminent, and let professionals take over for them. However, I have also seen this happen when well-meaning caregivers panic at the thought of death. They succumb to earlier conditioning which assumes that hospitals and professionals are needed to care for the dying properly. At this time sophisticated monitors and techniques are unnecessary. A hospital admission, and a family's untimely request that everything be done for their loved one, may result in more tests, treatments, and possibly surgery; interventions which are not in the best interests of the dying.

Get used to the idea that the best place to die is at home amid familiar surroundings. A USA Today survey revealed that a majority of the sick and elderly wanted to stay in their own homes until they died. The lowest score was for admission to a nursing home, which only five per cent chose. Home care for the dying is becoming more widely accepted, and the number of home care and hospice home care agencies is growing.

If you have no family to call on, and even with a family's help, the time may come when you need home care assistance and professional nursing help. Your physician can refer you to a home care agency or a hospice home care service, and to a social service agency for problems that arise regarding financial resources and insurance, or Medicare reimbursement.

HOME NURSING CARE

If you choose the help of a home care nursing agency, their social services director will investigate avenues of insurance or Medicare reimbursement for their services. Your own physician will continue to be in charge of your care. A registered nurse will come to your home to make your initial assessment and your written plan of care. She will communicate with your doctor whenever changes in your condition occur or questions arise. You can contact her with problems, or for advice and encouragement.

If your medical and personal needs escalate, she will arrange for a nursing assistant to come two or three times a week for personal cares such as bathing, skin and hair care, dressing changes, or catheter irrigation. Or you may need a home health aide who will bathe you, change your bed linen, do your personal laundry and light housekeeping.

Another option is a live-in home companion who will do the same things while living in your home. You must provide a separate room for her, and allow her weekends off, and eight hours daily to sleep.

Your registered nurse may assess that you need a physical or occupational therapist and, with your permission, will arrange for these visits also. She will contact home care supply agencies for oxygen therapy, a wheel chair or hospital bed, or any equipment which will make your life safer and more comfortable. This equipment is usually rented on a month to month basis.

HOSPICE HOME CARE

Certified hospice home care is a wise option when you and your doctor assess that death is approaching. To obtain Medicare or medical insurance coverage for hospice care, your physician must testify that you have six months or less to live. To utilize their services you may have to forego requests for resuscitation at time of death.

Even though you don't need their services immediately, it's wise to investigate these resources while you are alert and functioning, and let them know you may call on them in the future. If your physician is not available to make these referrals, contact your nearest hospice or hospital to make the arrangements.

At the time you request their services they will try to set up an assessment visit on the same day, always within twenty-four hours. A typical hospice home care service includes:

- a skilled, compassionate, response to physical pain issues, and symptom control.
- staff available to answer phone calls twenty-four hours a day, seven days a week.
- if necessary a staff member will visit within thirty to sixty minutes after you report a problem.
- staff members will respond honestly and sensitively to questions asked by patients and family members.
- staff will work to coordinate clear, effective communication among patient, family, and physicians, and supporting services.
- a support team member will be available for visits to assist with the psycho-social and spiritual concerns of families.
- providing care to patients is sometimes based on need rather than on ability to pay.

In most cases, hospice home care services require at least one full time person be living with you to insure that treatments and medications are given correctly, and at the right times. There have been notable exceptions. Arrangements have been made for terminal patients to live and die while remaining alone in their own homes. This requires the cooperation of family members, neighbors, visiting nurses, volunteers, and certified home health aides. At times the local police force has helped by checking on the person during the night.

If your pain or symptoms should get out of control, you can be admitted as an inpatient in the hospice unit on a temporary basis. Pain can be brought under control more quickly with round the clock nursing care, and your family can relax knowing you're in good hands.

Home care is the most desirable option, but despite the best of intentions and arrangements, things can go wrong that make it impossible. When thirty-four year old Gary reached the end stages of AIDS, he and his wife made plans to keep him at home throughout his illness and dying. Their two young children were also pleased to have Daddy at home with them.

But Gary developed a lymphoma on the frontal lobe of his brain, which grew rapidly and interfered with his mental capacities. He became confused and his actions and words became unpredictable. His wife was unable to control him and at times the children became frightened.

His doctor admitted him to the hospital to treat and hopefully shrink the tumor. In the process Gary developed a brain infection and it became clear that his condition would not stabilize and he could never return home. His doctor planned on keeping him in the intensive care unit, but an assisting physician intervened. He suggested that Gary be transferred to a hospice near his own home to spend his remaining days.

With his pain kept under control, and away from the noise and activity of the intensive care ward, Gary became calmer. His children were able to visit, and his wife spent most of her time in the hospice with him. Within one week he died in this peaceful atmosphere surrounded by his family.

You will find that in a hospice inpatient setting compassionate care is given with professional competency. Hospice medical directors specialize in pain management and have a back-up of medical and surgical specialists working with all types of incurable diseases, plus pharmacists, dieticians, psychologists, physical and occupational therapists, and Pastoral Care ministers for your spiritual needs. All work closely with your primary physician. Enough nursing staff and specially trained volunteers are on hand to provide all the extra attention that is needed to make you comfortable.

Respite Care is another valuable hospice service. If your family helpers need to take a break or go on a vacation, you can be admitted into an inpatient facility. They can relax, knowing you're in good hands. Five days of respite care are presently covered by

Medicare, however this is subject to frequent changes. If you have a private insurer be sure to inquire about their coverage for this service.

FINANCIAL ASSISTANCE

In my state of Wisconsin the Hospice Medicare Benefits program will presently cover 210 days of certified, licensed hospice services, plus medications which may require a minimal co-payment.   This includes at no cost to the patient:
- medications related to the terminal illness. (co-pay)
- durable medical equipment.
- in home medical supplies.
- home health aide/certified nurse assistant visits.
- therapy services including physical, occupational, respiratory, speech, ostomy, and dietary.
- short-term inpatient respite care to provide the primary caregiver a break from home care responsibilities.
- short-term hospitalization for pain or other symptom control.
- twenty-four hour home nursing care if required during a medical crisis.

This coverage is subject to change and differs in other localities, so it is best to check with your own state's Medicare office. This is one instance in which physicians need to predict how long you have to live, because they currently must testify that you have a terminal illness with six months or less to live in order to have you receive this service. Medicare covers about seven months of hospice care, after which alternative methods of payment must be found.

If you are not eligible for Medicare benefits, check the coverage of your private or work related medical insurance. Most health insurance companies now pay for home care and hospice services. If you lose your health insurance when you quit working you have the right to keep it effective with minimal payments for eighteen months under the Federal COBRA law. This is also subject to change.

If you find yourself in difficult financial straits and have no medical insurance or Medicare, there are a number of agencies that can assist you. Check with the following:

- your state disability program.
- Federal social security disability program.
- Federal supplementary security income program.
- your county and/or city welfare programs.

The systems of public financial and health related assistance are complex. You will need the help of the social service agency referral your doctor gives you. You may also need the help of your health partner, friend, or family member in filling out the large number of forms required.

A valuable source of information, referrals, and many other services can be obtained by calling the local and state agencies and organizations which are listed in the front of your phone directory: Department of Health, Department of Human Services, Department of Insurance, Meals on Wheels, Medicaid, Medicare, Office on Aging, and the Senior Resource Center in your community. Some directories have a Community Services listing at the front, which also contains valuable information for those in need.

Assistance for those who are alone:
Medic Alert Foundation
2323 Colorado
Turlock, CA 95381-1009
800-344-3226

Free publications on legal, financial, and medical aspects of health care: Order from AARP, 1909 K St. NW, Washington DC, 20049, or call 202-872-4700.

For information about local hospices or policies:
National Hospice Organization
1901 North Moore St., Suite 901
Arlington, VA, 22209 or call 703-243-5900.

Information for caregivers:

National Family Caregivers Association
9621 East Bexhill Drive
Kensington, MD 20895
800-896-3650

Well Spouse Foundation
P.O. Box 801
New York, NY 10023
800-838-0879

Additional Reading:

Andrea Sankar, "Dying at Home: A Family Guide to Caregiving", John Hopkins Univ. Press, 1991

Deborah Duda, "Coming Home: A Guide to Dying at Home with Dignity", Aurora Press, NY, 1987.

Larry Beresford, "The Hospice Handbook", Little Brown, 1993.

Edgar N. Jackson, "Talking About Death" A Dialogue Between Parent and Child", Beacon Press, Boston, 3rd Ed. 1990.

Jill Krementz, "How It Feels When a Parent Dies", Knopf, NY, 1983.

FOR CHILDREN:

Maryann Townsend & Ronnie Stern, "Pop's Secret", Addison-Wesley, Reading MA, 1980.

E. B. White, "Charlotte's Web", Harper Row, NY, 1952. Also available on video.

Kathleen C. Szaj, "I Hate Goodbyes", Paulist Press, NJ, 1996.

Robert Munsch, "Love You Forever", Firefly Books, Ontario, 36th printing, 1993.

Chapter VII
Your Rights

The plans you've been making involve the assistance of many other people and you may find yourself thinking, "I don't want to be such a bother to my friends or family members. After all, I'm dying so it doesn't really matter what happens to me." This is what I heard from my mother during her last months. She didn't even want us to bother cooking for her. In her final weeks she had just enough strength to lift herself unto her bedside commode, into her chair, and then back to bed.

"I'm no good for anything anymore," she would complain. We talked about the many ways she had helped us when she was young and strong. I told her how happy we were to have her special, loving presence in the midst of our family. I had to remind her many times that she was very important to us, and we enjoyed helping care for her.

You may begin wondering if it's fair to impose upon your family with this intrusion into their lives, and this disruption of their household, by choosing to die at home. Sometimes it may seem that you are placing a terrible burden on their shoulders, perhaps continuous twenty-four hour a day care. You might start to think about entering a nursing home, or a hospital or hospice, so your family can get on with their lives.

Choosing to die at home undoubtedly creates disruption in the household and in the family's routine. Nurturing a loved one during their illness and dying is a challenge for everyone involved. It is also a rare opportunity for them to show their love for you, by allowing you to die amid familiar and comfortable surroundings. Your being there shows them how they, too, can die amid the peace and beauty of a loving family when their time comes. Wouldn't you want to give them this opportunity to die at home if you were the caregiver and they were the sick ones?

All through our lives we are praised for 'doing things' and we forget that our real worth is in being who we are, a unique, irreplaceable human being. To help you overcome any 'worthless' feelings you may have, there is a copy of "The Dying Person's Bill of Rights" at the end of this chapter. Read your rights slowly and let them sink in.

THE RIGHT TO DIE

Along with your other rights you may wonder about the new trend to let people decide for themselves when and how they are to die. As more and more people demanded to have control over their own dying process, the "Living Will" became a legal option. We can choose what life-sustaining measures we do or don't want when our bodies are severely compromised.

Through the years, the sick and dying have discreetly ended their own lives by any means available, when living with an afflicted body became too great a strain on themselves and their caregivers. Sometimes relatives or doctors assisted them despite the threat of legal punishment.

The Netherlands has legalized the act of a physician prescribing a lethal dose of medication for patients, and instructing them how to take it themselves. In this country Dr. Kevorkian's physician assisted suicide was the most widely publicized intervention we have seen. Although the Supreme

Court ruled this illegal, he provided the means for suicides throughout the country before being indicted and imprisoned.

Arguments in favor of assisted suicide emphasize the need for quality of life. They include:

- Life must be self-supporting to have value.
- Life without ability to enjoy or create is worthless.
- People must be free to control their own dying.
- Controlling their own dying gives people more dignity.
- Death is preferable to living in pain.
- Death is preferable to mindless existence with Alzheimer's or senility.
- A lethal injection is more compassionate than removing a feeding tube and letting a patient starve to death.
- Death relieves caregivers and society of the expense and burden of caring for the terminally ill.

The arguments against legalized suicide emphasize a person's value and dignity at every stage of human life:

- Infants, the elderly, the infirm, and the mentally ill have intrinsic value during times when they are not self-supporting.

- Life is worth living even through periods when we cannot enjoy, create, or produce anything.
- People are created by God who determines their life span.
- Completing our developmental stage of dying enhances our dignity.
- Modern pain techniques can keep the dying comfortable.
- A person's inner soul and spirit are present, even when memory and rational thinking are gone.
- When the body is dying the sensations of hunger and thirst are no longer present, food and fluids are no longer needed.
- The dying, elderly, and infirm will feel pressured to use suicide to save society and caregivers the expense and trouble of caring for them.

This is by no means a complete list of all the arguments for and against assisted suicide, but it will give you an idea of what this conflict is all about. The 'slippery-slope' theory predicts that legalized assisted suicide would lead to the widespread practice of euthanasia, which is the systematic elimination of all non-productive members of society.

The Netherlands, where physician assisted suicide has been legal for several years, appears to be headed in this direction. This is what researchers have uncovered:

- in one year 1,000 people were 'assisted to death' without their prior request or consent. 80% of them were incompetent to make such a request. 20% were competent and did not request assisted suicide, but their doctors decided it was best for them. The courts ruled the doctors' actions were legal.

- one Catholic woman was assisted to die without prior knowledge; her doctor believed her faith would not allow her to request it, so he took the decision upon himself.

- This doctor and others were taken to court for not following the legal directives for assisted suicide; not one was indicted.

- an estimated four hundred newborn babies a year, with congenital anomalies such as Down's Syndrome, Spina Bifida, and heart defects, have been passively killed by withholding food and care.

- hospitals whose ethical standards do not allow such actions, found they could not legally prohibit them within their facility, nor were they allowed to discipline employees who took part in them.

- to protect themselves, some citizens carry preprinted cards on their person requesting they be allowed to live in case of sudden illness or accident.

The state of Oregon passed a law legalizing physician assisted suicide within its borders by the slim margin of 51% to 49%. Opponents of the law brought to light the abuses taking place in the

Netherlands, as well as dangerous loopholes in the Oregon statute. The slide down the "slippery slope" has begun.

The original law carefully limited assisted suicide to the act of prescribing lethal drugs which the patients themselves would take. An elderly man was too weak to accomplish this so his brother-in-law gave him the lethal injection. The brother-in-law was indicted, but the Attorney General ruled it would be unconstitutional and discriminatory to limit assisted suicide to those strong enough to perform the act themselves. It is now legal for anyone in Oregon to administer a lethal drug to persons presumably unable to take it themselves.

In 1997 the U.S. Supreme Court, in its ruling against physician-assisted suicide, re-emphasized the right of patients to withdraw life-sustaining equipment, including tubes for feeding and hydration. They emphasized the right of physicians to use any medications required to keep patients comfortable, even if it may cause them to die sooner. Patients also have the right to refuse life-sustaining interventions such as kidney dialysis, insulin therapy, and pacemakers.

My hope is that during your final illness you will be surrounded with so much love and compassion, receive such skilled care and pain control, that the thought of suicide will never enter your mind. The noted physician, Dr. Richard Lamerton, formerly of St.

Joseph's Hospice, said, "If anyone really wants euthanasia he must have pretty poor doctors and nurses. . . . . We as doctors have a duty so to care for our patients that they never ask to be killed off." 5

Additional Reading

George Burnell M.D., "Final Choices: To Live or Die in an Age of Medical Technology", Insight Plenum Press, N.Y., 1993.

Sherwin Nuland, "How We Die", Alfred A. Knopf, N.Y., 1994.

Judith Ahronheim M.D. & Doron Weber, "Final Passages: Positive Choices for the Dying and their Loved Ones", Simon & Schuster, N.Y., 1992.

THE DYING PERSON'S BILL OF RIGHTS

I have the right to be treated as a living human being
until I die.

I have the right to maintain a sense of hopefulness,
however changing its focus might be.

I have the right to be cared for by those who can
maintain a sense of hopefulness, however
changing this might be.

I have the right to express my feelings and emotions
about my approaching death in my own way.

I have the right to participate in decisions about my
care.

I have the right to expect continuing medical and
nursing attention, even though "cure" goals
must be changed   to "care" goals.

I have the right not to die alone.

I have the right to have my questions answered
honestly.

I have the right not to be deceived.

I have the right to have help from and for my family in
accepting my death.

I have the right to die in peace and dignity.

I have the right to retain my individuality and not be
judged for my decisions which may be contrary
to the beliefs of others.

I have the right to expect that the sanctity of the human
body will be respected after my death.

I have the right to be cared for by caring, sensitive,
knowledgeable people who will attempt to
understand my needs, and will be able to gain
some satisfaction in helping me face my death.
Marilee Donovan & Sandra Pierce. 1976. Cancer
Care Nursing, New York: Appleton Century Crofts,
p.33.
To these I would add: I have the right to receive the
spiritual care and comfort I desire.

Chapter VIII
Calming Emotional Storms

What does it mean to die with dignity? Our goal is to meet all of our days in full possession of our individuality and our dignity, in a manner of our own choosing. This doesn't mean we must force ourselves to put up a good front and act dignified no matter what. To do so during times of illness and stress would be emotionally unhealthy.

It's okay if your house gets dusty, your hair mussed, your clothes get wrinkled, or if you feel ornery and forget to say "please" and "thank you". You'll have good days when you'll want to take care of all these things. Days when you enjoy a task you're working on, feel love and gratitude for your care-givers, feel positive about yourself and the remainder of your life. You'd like the rest of your days to feel this good.

Bad days come when your body finds a new way to hurt, a new sore or lump, a cramp or ache in an unexpected place. They also come when there isn't any bad thing you can identify but something inside you boils up in irrational anger, irritability, gloom, fear, desperation, envy, jealousy, humiliation, or hope-lessness. Sometimes you feel like a yo-yo on the end of a string of conflicting emotions and mood swings.

Your life has gone through dramatic changes since your illness was diagnosed. Even when you've made the external adjustments, there remains the task of re-evaluating who you are, what your life is worth now, and how your relationships with others have changed. These tasks, demanding your attention, disturb your inner peace and heave emotions to the surface. Anticipate them by finding out what they mean and how they work, and by planning a few strategies to calm them down.

In her book, "On Death and Dying" Dr. Elisabeth Kubler-Ross found it helpful to sort out this array of conflicting emotions and classify them into five main stages of grief (and you are grieving over what you've lost and are still losing): denial, anger, bargaining, depression, and acceptance. 6   These psychological reactions come into play whenever we suffer a loss. We find that they are not so much stages, as they are outward manifestations of our inner struggle to understand and accept the truth of our present condition. They don't march by in orderly fashion, but tumble over us in waves that go back and forth and get mixed together. Some are more prevalent in the early stages of illness and others near the end.   Some persons may skip a stage entirely, and experience others more frequently.

DENIAL

Occasionally, I found myself caring for persons who maintained an attitude of denial throughout their illness. Although they would not verbally admit to the fact that they were dying, I sensed they were aware of the truth. Perhaps they needed this pretense to avoid the developmental tasks of 'letting go', or perhaps to eliminate painful goodbyes.

The staff was careful to respect their wishes as long as they didn't request inappropriate treatments. Sometimes their physicians had to speak with them frankly about why an additional treatment wouldn't help, or why resuscitation at time of death would not be useful for them. As caregivers, we had to remind ourselves that their way of denial was not a 'wrong' way to die. Each person is free to choose his or her own 'best' way.

Denial usually surfaces right at the beginning with the refusal to believe a life-threatening diagnosis. Denial can return later in an irrational conviction that your disease has abated and you are cured. Sometimes you simply need these periods of denial to give yourself a brief respite from dealing with your illness, and to keep you going. Kubler-Ross describes a woman who believed her tumors had disappeared through the use of alternative healing methods. After a brief period of 'wellness' the disease returned with a vengeance. 7

Hope is good, and sometimes healings have been documented which no doctor or scientist can explain. Are these miracles or a bodily process we don't understand? How often should we hope for a miracle?

When Roger C. Bone, M.D. was stricken with widespread metastatic cancer after a long career as a pulmonary and critical care physician, he began filling notebooks with reflections about his illness. He describes the tortuous, and many times painful journey through his stages of grief; resolving his conflicts, letting go, and finally his acceptance as death approached.

What he found surprising was that even though his lifelong career was based on scientific and clinical observations, throughout his terminal illness he never lost a tiny flicker of hope that some miracle or scientific breakthrough would restore him to health. What he discovered was that the final stage of acceptance, and a small spark of hope in one's heart, could co-exist peacefully right up to the ending of bodily life. Dr. Bone's miracle never materialized, but he did find peace in achieving his 'best' way to die.

ANGER

We all have legitimate reasons to be angry at times, and there will be even more reasons during a prolonged illness. For one thing, our medical system is fraught with bureaucratic bungling. Your treatments may be rescheduled for less convenient times, or you may rush to be on time for your doctor's appointment, then wait for an hour while he sees the patients ahead of you. Or you might find that your doctors or nurses are not available when you need them.

If you are dependent on others for your shopping, you may have to wait several days for what you want, or end up with the wrong item. Visitors you were expecting don't always come on time, and some don't show up at all. It's much harder to cope with all these annoyances when you don't feel well.

Besides these obvious frustrations there are more subtle angers directly related to having a life-threatening illness. Our inborn 'fright, fight, or flight' mechanism prompts us to lash out at something or someone when we feel threatened. In a severe illness our enemy is our disease, and it's not clear to whom or what we should direct our anger. When anger shoots out in the wrong direction it's called 'displaced anger'.

In the hospice I saw an elderly man make a fist and sock my co-worker in the jaw while she bathed him. One woman would slap my hands every time I brought her medication. One of Kubler-Ross' clients, a mother whose five year-old was dying from a brain tumor, ashamedly admitted to having angry feelings toward the child who was causing her so much work and anguish. 8

Displaced anger originates with you, and with your caregivers and family members alike, building up steam as it goes back and forth. To prevent a raging battle and the breakup of relationships, everyone involved can:

-Look for tangible causes for anger such as: increased pain, major physical setback, financial worries, overwork and strain. Take steps to alleviate these.
-Recognize the emotion for what it is, 'displaced anger' a product of everyone's grief and frustration.
-Work out anger in non-destructive ways. We had a room off the main wing where patients could cry out, wail, shout, or swear without disturbing others.

-Exercise if you have the strength for it, walk outside, or request a wheelchair ride in a park. Nature's green, sunshine, and fresh air are calming.

-Write down angry thoughts and describe how you feel in a notebook. No one has to see it unless you want them to.

-Talk to a neutral party about anger, yours and others.

-When there is no one to talk with, pour out your thoughts unto a tape recording.

-Reread Chapter III on how to open dialogue about sensitive feelings. Ask those whom you perceive as angry at you to read it also, and then set up discussion times.

Many of us have been taught to think of anger as socially unacceptable. Raised as a devout Christian I was taught to believe it was sinful. But untreated anger must have an outlet, and we have found sneaky ways to let it out through passive/aggressive acts like:

-'Accidentally' spilling or breaking something so others have to clean up the mess. (Don't confuse this with unavoidable weakness or shakiness.)

-'Forgetting' to relay phone or other messages, or twisting the message to confuse someone or make them feel hurt.

-Finding words or ways to make others feel guilty or incompetent.

-Projecting our own anger on others, thus making them seem like the angry ones.

-Persistent generalized anger at the medical staff or institution, at the government, the church, racial minorities, and so on.

-Deliberately missing appointments, treatments, 'forgetting' to take our medications.

-Loss of faith and/or inability to pray because of buried anger at God.

ANGER AT GOD

Ferret out these subtle anger symptoms and deal with them in the manner described above. Admitting to anger at God is a scary prospect for a person of faith, seemingly blasphemous and worthy of condemnation. As an example, when my oldest son, Philip, died I could no longer pray. "How could You let this happen to him? Why did You let him die? We trusted You. How could You do this to us?" was all that would come to my mind.

This went on for months until the night that such a rage built up inside of me that I went into what used to be the nursery, closed the door and looked down at the spot where his crib had stood. I screamed and shouted at God for a long time accusing Him of deliberately hurting me, hurting my son, betraying my trust, demanding to know 'why'. I was in such a fury I didn't care if He struck me dead.   When my anger was exhausted I fell into a deep sleep.

God did not strike me dead, and after that, to my surprise, prayer came easily. God allowed me to feel His own compassion and sorrow at my distress, which at one point felt as though He were crying with me. He opened my understanding to the discrepancies in our human nature, and the conflicts caused by free will. I felt much closer to God than I had before our tragedy, and I began to heal.

If you are angry at God don't be afraid to tell Him so. You can speak frankly to Him because He knows your innermost thoughts and every nuance of your feelings, even the ones you have trapped in your subconscious.   He is both the most merciful and solicitous of fathers and the most loving and compassionate of mothers. He will help and comfort you if you let Him in.

BARGAINING

One of the more obvious strategies of the incurably ill is making bargains with the doctor, caregivers, and mostly with God. They ask for a cure or a little more time in exchange for a promise such as donating all their money to charity, or living an exemplary life, or resigning themselves to die at a later date.   Such promises are rarely kept.

Some encounter bargaining strategies in dreams of being made well under certain conditions, such as never being able to leave their house, or being able to look at their loved ones only through a window. As silly as these bargaining dreams seem on awakening, they serve to release some of the internal conflict of the dreamer.

By the time people reached our hospice they'd found out bargains didn't work, but I still heard pleadings such as: "Just help me get well enough to take my sister to that new French Bistro for her birthday," or "My husband and I made travel plans. If we could just take one trip together I'd come back and die in peace." One bargain did succeed, "If I could go to my daughter's wedding Saturday I wouldn't mind coming back here." Her family took her in a wheel chair with a portable oxygen tank and she made it through the whole day. She died a few weeks later.

DEPRESSION

For many years depression has been explained as anger turned inward against ourselves. More recent research recognizes it as a separate emotion of extreme, persistent sadness which does not abate. At the core of most terminally ill persons dwells a persistent, yet manageable note of sadness. I found that depression sometimes lifts when pain and distressing symptoms are brought under control, but it is very rare for those facing death, and the prospect of losing everything, not to experience some periods of depression.

Help your loved ones understand how they can support you in dealing with your depression. Let them know they don't have to cheer you up. Unlike early depression at the beginning of your illness, this is not the time for funny stories and positive thinking. You need to go through the sadness, experience the heaviness of it, bear with the emotional pain for now, because it is leading you to your next stages, 'letting go' and acceptance. Friends and family can help you best by just being there, sitting quietly with you, holding your hand, letting you talk if you need to.

I encountered a more immobilizing depression in some of our patients, which prevented them from carrying out even the simplest activities of daily living. They were too weak to seek help or even understand the symptoms of depression. If family, caregivers, or medical staff advise you to get help for depression, please do so, for they see something in you that you may be too sick to recognize.

Confusion in medical practice has sometimes classified depression in the dying as 'mental illness' and over-treated it with tranquilizers and mood elevators. Mild anti-depressants can be helpful, but over-medicating can rob you of working through your dying, and healing your inner conflicts. The counseling of therapists or clergymen, and healing interactions with caregivers, loved ones, and God, can guide you through a natural grieving process as you come to terms with your losses.

TECHNIQUES THAT HEAL EMOTIONS

To obtain some relief from the ups and downs of your emotions you may find it helpful to practice relaxation techniques. Hospice staff are trained to facilitate this but those of you at home can easily learn it yourself. A good method of relaxation consists of getting into a comfortable sitting or lying down position and, starting with your feet and working up, progressively tighten your muscles then let them go limp, until all the parts of your body relax. Playing soft repetitive strains of some of the New Age music facilitates the relaxed mood. If you prefer, you can obtain recorded cassettes of relaxation exercises at bookstores and music stores.

You can follow up relaxation with Creative Imaging. Creative Imaging is an excellent psychological technique developed in the 1970's for lifting our spirits or calming us down. We can use our imaginations and our memories to put ourselves in pleasant places and happy situations. The things one sees in the mind's eye are as real, in one sense, as the things one sees through a window. There is not much difference between the healing signals activated by imagination and memory and the ones that are activated by the eye itself. Again, guided imagery is available on cassettes.

Creative activities are also good outlets for relieving disturbing thoughts and feelings. You may have a creative hobby such as photography, bird watching, painting, modeling clay, or writing poetry, short stories, or your autobiography. Or you may want to try something new. Kubler-Ross tells of a hospice resident who used his carpentry skills to build a doll house for his grandchildren, then went on to make the furniture to put in it. 9

DREAMS

Your subconscious mind is also working to calm emotional conflicts through healing dreams. Our hospice patients found that as their physical abilities diminished, their intuitive and spiritual awareness grew, resulting in the frequent occurrences of healing dreams. In her book "On Dreams and Death", Marie Louise VonFranz cites the research on dreams of the dying done by the psychologist, Carl Jung. Shortly before they died people reported the following types of dreams which helped them resolve their conflicts and led them to acceptance and peace. 10

- Packing suitcases to go on an exciting adventure.

- Awakening in a beautiful place; given the choice to stay or return home.
- Promised a reward for living a good life.
- Caught a glimpse of a beautiful new world.
- A beautiful young man or woman came to embrace them.
- Visited with deceased loved ones.
- Watched the sprouting and regrowing of burnt forests, harvested wheat or corn.
- Went through a dark passage to emerge in a love filled bright light.
- Filled with beautiful sights and feelings of ecstasy.

A friend of mine in his twenties, nearing the end of his university studies was diagnosed with Leukemia. For several years he struggled to overcome the physical and emotional trauma the disease caused him. He described the following healing dream: "I was looking over the edge of a high cliff into the dark water of a vast lake. The entire lake was surrounded by banks so high and steep that I knew if anyone fell into it they could never get out and would drown.

"It was night and heavy clouds blocked all light from moon or stars but as my eyes adjusted to the darkness I began to see thousands of tiny lights from the windows of houses all around the clifftop. I sensed that the whole human race was contained in these houses, including my family, my friends, and myself.

"In a flash of illumination I saw that eventually we were all going to fall into that lake, which was symbolic of the waters of death, and from that moment on I felt a kinship with the whole scope of human tragedy. I saw the manner in which we all start our life's journey expecting it to flow in a predictable continuum, a normal pattern of daily experiences, then, suddenly, we are struck by an 'off-time event', a 'discontinuous change' of all our expectations and plans.

"When I awakened from this dream I had the inner peace which comes to those who accept the realities of life and death, and I lost the conviction that I had been singled out and stricken by my dreadful disease. At last I could stop asking, 'why me?' because I knew this fate was not mine alone, but everyman's condition, and that sooner or later tragedy and death happen to all." Through that dream and others the young man gained inner peace and acceptance of his condition.

Additional Reading

William Bridges, "Transitions: Making Sense of Life's Changes", Addison-Wesley, Menlo Park, 1980.

Jeremy Taylor, "Where People Fly and Water Runs Uphill: Using Dreams to Tap the Wisdom of the Unconscious", Warner Books, N. Y., 1992.

Carol Tavris, "Anger: The Misunderstood Emotion", Simon & Schuster, 1984.

Chapter IX
Support Groups

Perhaps you'd like to find out what techniques are helping others who have your disease, or maybe you feel the need to share what you are going through with those who'll understand what it's like. One of the powerful tools available to all of us with difficulties to sort out is the Support Group.

These groups are especially valuable if you have few relatives or close friends who can spend time with you on a regular basis. Then, too, as compassionate and caring as your loved ones may be, they are not experiencing the effects of your disease nor facing the same challenges that you are. Some of the advantages of joining a group of people who are struggling with the same disease are:

- Sharing your painful experiences with them lets you know it's okay to think and feel the way you do.
- Listening to others' experiences gives you a better understanding of what is happening to you.
- Learning how others deal with problems will give you clues to overcoming your own.
- You may obtain information and insight about your disease that is not available in books, or is unknown to your caregivers.
- Opening your heart to the suffering of those around you takes your mind off yourself.
- Obtain comfort for yourself when fellow sufferers show their care and concern for you.

In hospital and hospice settings I witnessed the importance of 'support systems' in the recovery of any sick person. Even when a cure is not possible, healing of emotional and physical pain is facilitated by the kind of caring and sharing you can receive in a support group. Statistics show that the terminally ill who take part in such groups tend to live longer than those who don't. An extended life period, however, is an added benefit of the healing such participation brings, so if you stick with a support group that doesn't feel right for you just to live longer it probably won't work.

A word of caution is in order here. Support group enthusiasts may pressure you to join a group which has helped them or someone they know. Don't think you must take part in it, or in any group, in order to find healing. Only join a group if *you* feel the need for it.

Your doctor, social worker, therapist, or medical facility can help you find the groups who are afflicted with your illness. Or you can check your newspaper, church bulletin, the National Society for your disease, or the Health and Human Services listings in your phone book.

If you have a choice of support groups near you, make inquiries to see if there is one in which participants are in your particular stage of illness. For instance, if you have just been diagnosed HIV positive, it would probably be too depressing to join a support group of advanced stage AIDS sufferers. Or, if you are in supportive care for metastatic cancer, you would not have much to learn from cancer patients who are just beginning treatment.

If you are not sure that a particular support group, or any support group, is right for you, ask the group facilitator if you can sit in on a meeting. You can then listen to the flow of conversation, the give and take of ideas and feelings, without having to participate. Afterwards ask yourself the following questions:

- Did you feel you shared a common ground with the members?
- What feelings did their sharing evoke in you: anger, grief, sadness, compassion?
- Do you feel okay about these emotions and about sharing them with this group?
- Were any of the group members blamed, manipulated, coerced?
- What did you want to say or ask during the meeting?
- How did you feel when the meeting ended?
- Are you anxious to attend another meeting or do you hate the thought of going again?

If you decide to join a group you'll find that although you are all sharing the same incurable disease, each member has a unique viewpoint in facing problems. Accept each person's individual expressions of his/her own living and dying experience even though it differs from your own. Let go of preconceived ideas of how they should act, or how you should act. Each of you will:

- Tell your own story of life-threatening illness.
- Share your own needs and emotions.
- Search for your own unfinished business.

- Find and let go of negative feelings that sap your energy, such as guilt and fear.
- Work toward an unconditional acceptance of yourself and each other.

National Societies for specific diseases can be found in the directory at the back of the book.

Additional Reading:

Bernie Siegel, "Peace, Love, and Healing", Harper & Row, NY, 1989.

Chapter X
Letting Go

Your life has changed drastically since that day your illness was diagnosed. Sometimes it seems that all you were at that time, all you had worked hard to accomplish, all your gains and possessions, are like so much water slipping away through your cupped hands. Up until then your tasks in life were gathering the skills, knowledge, expertise, jobs, control, possessions, and relationships necessary to make your life successful and rewarding.

Now you have come to your developmental task of dying, and that task is recognizing, appreciating, loving, and being thankful for all the good things you had, and then letting them go. Although you thought these lifetime gains would last forever, they were only yours to keep while you needed them.   As you gradually put aside their importance you will begin to notice the value of other good things that are flowing in to fill the void.

LETTING GO OF POSSESSIONS
You have already arranged for the transfer of your possessions to your loved ones. Be grateful you had something to give them because many leave the world with nothing to bestow. Even if you have few material possessions you have left them the legacy of your life and an example of living well until you die.

When they died within a week of each other, Princess Diana left an estate of two million pounds, and Mother Teresa of Calcutta left a change of clothes, a pair of sandals, and a wooden bucket. Yet each, in her own way, left a legacy of caring for the poor and suffering of this world, and the motivation for the rest of us to do the same.

Every day you hear on the news about the fires, floods, and earthquakes that destroy people's homes and all their possesions. Last month my elderly friend's house was burglarized and she came home to find her telephones, television, stereo, clothes, her grandmother's sterling silver service, antique crystal, and jewelry, treasures of a lifetime, all gone without a moment's notice. All our material possessions have been at risk since the day we acquired them, and we've been fortunate to have enjoyed them this long. Still, when they're gone we grieve for the loss of them.

During months of living with a difficult illness, you're discovering that what you really need is the sunshine, a walk through your garden, the smell of fresh cut grass, a chocolate bar, the laughter of children, a hot cup of coffee, your favorite tune playing on the stereo, a symphony, the smiles of your loved ones, the touch of your spouse's hand. These have always been the most important things in your life and you get to keep most of them right up to the end.

LOSS OF CONTROL

You used to have control over your body, your mobility, your work, your time schedule, your recreation, and sometimes your children. Now there are days when you can't control your bodily functions, nor who you are going to be with and for how long, when or what you will eat, or what time you get up or go to bed. More and more you've been having to trust so many people to provide almost everything you need.

It seems like a strange and fearful thing to possess practically no control over anything. However, much of what you thought of as control before was an illusion. Your well being has always been in the hands of many others whom you've had to trust.

All of us are subject to government and the laws of the land, and we must trust that our leaders will govern with prudence and integrity,   that they will not precipitate a nuclear war, or that the Internal Revenue Service will not lock us up for non-payment of taxes we never owed.

We trust that our place of employment will not go bankrupt and close its doors tomorrow, or that a crazed terrorist will not blow up the entire building with us in it. We trust that our mechanic adjusted our brakes properly and they won't fail when we need them, or that the passing motorist will not lose control and swerve into us. We trust that the prescription drug we rely on was mixed correctly, or that our daughter's hamburger does not contain a deadly bacteria.

There are some immediate circumstances that you can control right now, like the treatments you choose, making sure you get enough pain medication, the TV shows you watch, the topics you discuss, the books you read, the music you listen to. In fact, most of the time *you* are in control of your caregivers who are on hand to serve your needs.

A good exercise to help incorporate the feeling of 'letting go' is allowing your caregivers to start making some of the decisions for you. Try saying to them, "Why don't you choose which outfit I should wear today?" Learning to trust will enhance your peace when you come to the time of being unable to direct your care, perhaps even being unable to speak. And it's good practice for when the time comes for your spirit to depart from your body and you must entrust yourself to a passage into the next world.

FORGIVING, FORGETTING, RE-EVALUATING

You've had plenty of time to review your life and most likely you'll see places where it has fallen short of what you wished you'd have been, done, said, seen, or not done, or not said. Remember, you didn't know then as much as you know now. Most of us do pretty well with the knowledge, insights, strengths, weaknesses, resources, and circumstances available at the time of a particular action. If you have difficulty letting go of past mistakes, meannesses, or lost opportunities, try writing them out in a journal.

I chastised myself bitterly for not being a better mother after my son, Philip, committed suicide. I began writing about his life in minute detail, focusing on every harsh scolding or criticism I'd inflicted on him, every foolish reply I'd ever made, all those things he wanted that I refused to buy or provide for him, those times he wanted my help but I was too busy.

When I read the journal later I realized that the interactions were mostly the normal give and take of any parent/child relationship, and as a friend I shared it with pointed out, I had other children, a husband, and a house to take care of at that time. It's easy to forget all the pressures we had in our life when we zoom in on one particular mistake.

If writing is too tiring, get a tape recorder and talk out all of your regrets into it. Talk about your whole life while you're at it, not forgetting the good parts. When you play it back even the sound of your own voice will be a surprise, and you will see yourself and your life in a new light. You will see your life is a mixed bag of successes and failure, joys and disappointments, love and hate, good deeds and bad deeds.

Now tell this person on the tape that you forgive all the mistakes and are ready to forget them. Then give yourself a pat on the back, and a hug besides, and be grateful for the good, the beautiful, the loving accomplishments of your life. You can either throw the recording away or pass it along as a memorial for the loved ones you leave behind. Many people are now making video recordings of their parting messages as a final gift to loved ones.

When your body is ready to shut down but you have some important issue to resolve, or a relationship to reconcile, you will struggle to hang on until your conflict is settled. That's why it's important to take care of all unfinished business well ahead of time. If you've been harboring a grudge for a long time, or are angry at someone over a recent injury, try reviewing it in the light of what you have learned about yourself.

Forgiving is mostly a matter of understanding the person, the incident, the reasons. Sometimes we don't feel like we can forgive, or maybe we're not sure. If you rarely think about the incident and are able to get on with your living and dying you've probably resolved it. If you find yourself thinking continually about the hurt or the injurer to the detriment of your peace, talk to your clergyman, your therapist, a friend you can trust, and pray, placing the matter and the person in God's hands.

LETTING GO OF LOVED ONES

As your physical abilities decline you will find yourself losing interest in social encounters, the affairs of your world, even the daily activities of friends and family members. You are centering into the affairs of your heart, learning about the hidden wealth within your own spirit, and it becomes of growing interest to you. You are moving from your present plane of physical existence to the purely psychological and spiritual.

The awareness may overtake you that you have been a pilgrim traveling in a foreign land and the people you know are fellow tourists. You're ready to say goodbye to them but you sense you'll run into them again some day. You realize now that the spirits of those who love each other are never separated. Some days you will enjoy having your loved ones around, and at other times you'll need your privacy. If others tend to hover about too much, tell them you need some time alone to sort out your thoughts and meditate.

Sensitive persons find it hard to tell others, "I need to be alone now." The openness and truth you've been striving for throughout your illness will help now. Communicate your new urges to draw into yourself, to find healing in your own soul. Tell loved ones about the fading importance of places, people, and everyday chit-chat going on about you, because you have your spiritual eyes on a new horizon. Sharing your changing self with them will help them to understand why you sometimes withdraw from them, and it will help them to let go of you at the end.

You've been letting go of your material world and are preparing to withdraw from the physical presence of your loving earthly relationships. It's just as important for your loved ones to prepare themselves to let go of you.

I witnessed a mother dying of ALS brought back to consciousness by her three teen-aged sons who cried at her bedside and begged her to come back. When she revived she asked them, "Why did you bring me back? I was in a place of sunshine, beautiful green fields and flowers. I felt so peaceful, so happy." We counseled the sons about letting go, and when their mother lapsed into unconsciousness again they cried quietly and let her go.

OPENING TO THE SPIRIT

Perhaps in reviewing your life you wondered why you chose this path instead of that one, were fascinated by this subject and not that one. Maybe you chose to do things no one in your family ever did before. Everyone of us possesses a vast depth of spirituality which guides our way of being and acting in this world in the light of love and ultimate values. People of faith recognize this spiritual guide all their lives and learn to work with it. Others discover the spiritual force within them when a dramatic or traumatic event blows away enough surface distraction to reveal it. Some find that deep place of ultimate truth when they are dying.

Almost everyone who works thoughtfully through their dying stage of development is attracted to this deep place of spiritual abiding ever more frequently. Some resist it because of previous conditioning or a death-blow to the spirit received sometime during their life. Others with scientific orientation can believe only in biological realities. Even in science there is room for doubt, and perhaps it's possible to at least stay open to the chance that spirit, and life after death, are real.

It is natural at this time to desire communication with the spiritual to develop deeper understanding, and to gain a closer union with this eternal abiding that attracts us. Depending on your culture and religious (or non-religious) upbringing, this will be God, Yahweh, Jesus, Buddha, The Great Spirit, or a vague force, power, or creator. However the dying relate to it, the presence feels familiar, the place they are being drawn to feels like home.

To pray for deeper understanding and a closer union, a few simple words of recognition, wonder, gratitude, or petition will do just fine. Caregivers can play religious hymns or read familiar passages from the bible, or spiritual books of other faiths, to aid in meditation, but this is not the time for lengthy prayers or flowery phrases. When you become too weak to concentrate on prayer, a single chosen word or mantra repeated at the end of each breath keeps you in touch with your eternal home.

THE CLOSURE

Near the end you will need more rest, you'll begin to sleep much of the time. Before you lose consciousness you may want to arrange for some special prayers you'd like said when the time comes for your spirit to leave your body.

Your sense of hearing will be the last of your senses to fade, so you may hear what others are saying even when you appear to be asleep. As your metabolism slows down, so does your desire for food or drink. A swab to keep your mouth and lips from drying out feels good and is all you need at this time.

As your circulation slows down, the decrease in oxygen to your brain diminishes your bodily sensations and enhances your sleepiness with a sense of peace. Sometimes an unexplained high fever develops which further increases your sleepiness. Your caregivers may feel better placing cool, moist cloths on your forehead, or giving you suppositories to lower your temperature. Your feet and legs may become cold to the touch, but you will scarcely feel it. Even so, your caregivers will keep them bundled up for you. Changes in metabolism and circulation may stimulate repetitive reflex motions in your body. Soft music, the downward stroking of a loved one's hand particularly on your forearms, or the gentle massage of your palm helps calm them down.

Your rhythmic breathing will become irregular, then change to seconds of no breathing followed by a deep breath. You may begin to make a gurgling sound with each breath as your tissues fill with fluid, but you won't notice because you'll already be more in the spirit world than in your body. If it disturbs those around your bedside, they can help by elevating your head or gently turning you on your side. It's important for them to maintain an aura of peacefulness as your spirit leaves your body.

Villagers in Eastern Europe open all their doors and windows when someone dies so the spirit can depart, and some Mexican cultures had a practice of cutting a hole in their roofs at this time. This is just symbolic because doors, windows, and roofs will not be barriers for your departing spirit.

LIFE AFTER LIFE

In her new book "The Wheel of Life" Dr. Kubler-Ross identifies four stages of 'life after life' she has gleaned from past interviews with thousands of her dying patients, many of whom had near death experiences. Her belief in the truth of these testimonies is unshakable.

Briefly in **Phase I**; People have already left their bodies and are witnessing their deathbed scene. **Phase II**; They are now spirit and energy and are comforted by guides who help them understand what's happening. **Phase III**; A passage over a bridge, a river, or through a tunnel, to a brilliant comforting light which reveals to them that the meaning of all life is love. **Phase IV**; In the presence of a higher source, filled with all knowledge, they review their entire life in the light of unconditional love.   All agree this review was non-condemning and not frightening. 11

My husband and I were awakened at 2:00 a.m. one night by a phone call, "This is Kenosha Memorial Hospital.   Your son, Christopher, has been in a car accident. He's in our Emergency Department." To my frantic inquiries the same dispassionate voice replied, "He's in critical condition."

During the hour long drive, I stared at the deserted stretch of highway unrolling before us, imagining how Chris might look; bloody, bruised, hooked up to the tubes and wires of life support systems.   Suddenly I was enveloped by the feeling and warmth of his presence. I imagined I heard his voice calling, "Mom". An overwhelming tenderness welled up in me, and I cradled his presence in my arms, whispering the first words that came to my mind.   "You're okay Chris, you're going to be okay. Don't be afraid. I love you. God loves you." For a few seconds I clung to him, then he was gone. The whole encounter lasted less than a minute.

I thought Chris was somehow reaching out to me for comfort in his suffering. I urged Harry to drive faster. "Chris needs us," I told him. When we arrived at the hospital, we found out that Chris had died over an hour earlier. He was already dead when we got the phone call.

Eight years later, while researching Near Death Experiences, I found the explanation for that mystical visit with my son. When people die suddenly, their newly released spirits are puzzled by what is happening to them. They seek out someone they love and trust to obtain guidance. I know now that Christopher's spirit had come to me that night for reassurance.

Much research has been done on Near Death Experiences and many explanations proposed for them. In 1973 Dr. Raymond Moody wrote down the testimonies of one hundred fifty people who returned from the other world. 12   Many other books and testimonies have been written since then by people who've had such a 'near death experience'. We may choose to believe or not believe these were actual glimpses of the afterlife that awaits us. What I find most comforting is the fact that the people who took part in these interviews said they'd had a wondrous experience, and now they are not afraid to die. Doctor Kubler-Ross, after witnessing thousands of deaths and interviewing a vast number of dying people, says she is looking forward to dying.

Additional Reading

Gail Perry & Jill Perry, "A Rumor of Angels: Quotations for Living, Dying, and Letting Go, Ballantine, N.Y., 1989.

Lewis B. Smedes, "Forgive and Forget", Simon and Schuster, 1986.

Stephine Levine, "Who Dies?", Anchor Press, NY 1982.

Joan Borysenko, "Pocketful of Miracles", Interfaith meditations, Warner Books, 1994.

A. J. Russell, "God Calling", Non-denominational Christian meditations, Dodd, Mead, & Co., N.Y., 22nd printing 1987.

Raymond Moody M.D., "Life after Life", Mockingbird Press, Covington GA., 1975.

Betty J. Eadie, "Embraced by the Light", Gold Leaf Press, CA, 1992.

Chapter XI
For Those Left Behind

As my godson, David, observed, "It's not a bad thing to die and go to heaven. What makes it hard is that we don't all go together." For those of us who remain, there exists a jagged wound in that deep and hidden place from which our loved one was torn. Although we can't see them, wounds of grief are as real as any physical wound, and often take longer to heal. Our cuts and skin tears heal faster if a doctor closes them with stitches, and our broken bones mend straight when set properly by an orthopedist. To resolve our grief, we need the attention of those who know how to guide and support the bereaved.

If you've been paying close attention to your loved one throughout the illness and dying, shared in the grieving, accepted the letting go, and talked out all your goodbyes, half of your grief work is done. Many guides, support groups, and books are available to help you get through what remains. It is wisdom to seek their help and take care of yourself now, because grief that is ignored or buried does not disappear. It will fester and trouble you for the remainder of your life.

How long will you grieve? The reply must be the same as when you asked how long your loved one would live. Every person, every situation, is fraught with variables. My personal experience is that it seems to last too long. Well-intentioned people may tell you, "You ought to be done grieving by now." I've read clinical books telling me at what month to part with my loved one's belongings, on what day I should return to work, and what year I should be finished grieving. Don't believe them. You will work out your own time table, and it will be the best for you.

Another scary phrase I've heard is, "You're never going to get over this." Not true. You will always miss the old days you shared with your loved one, and feel a pinch of sadness when you think of your loss. But it is a gentle sadness. The searing pain of separation and grinding ache of loss, will heal if you take time to work through your grief now.

To give you a glimpse of what it feels like to grieve, my daughter has allowed me to share the reflections she wrote after her brothers, Philip and Christopher died.

* * *

"September 25th. I used to know about death. Let's see, who died - both grandfathers, one grandmother, great aunts and uncles, a cousin, a few childhood friends, the family dog, numerous cats, birds, fish (hundreds), hamsters, hermit crabs, and houseplants. But now I don't know about death. My brother killed himself this day.

I never before wrote down these memories because it's not necessary. I'll never forget. I was lying down upstairs around three o'clock in the afternoon, when a man came to the door. He spoke with my mother and I heard an odd sound, a sound that wasn't right, like a cat crying outside in the night. I went downstairs and found my sister hugging/supporting my mother, both crying. My mother spoke, "Phil's dead."

If there's one place where all the emotions are kept, it was as if someone had removed that part of me - an emotionectomy, of sorts. I know I was crying at the time, but I didn't know where the tears came from. I felt nothing. I thought 'no'.

This is what grief means to me. Grief is going to my parent's house that evening and listening to my mother call my brothers and sisters. She repeated the same story over and over and over again, always letting out a sob when she got to the line "Phil's dead." With every repetition, I too would begin to cry and it became a little more real.

Grief is forgetting to eat and forgetting to drink. Lying awake at night, knowing you're not crying, yet feeling tears streaming down your face. Sitting in one place for hours that feel like minutes, unable to move.

But from the instant I learned of his death, I also began to heal. I felt like a burn victim. As the nerves began to heal, my feelings began to return, more sensitive than ever before. But when these feelings did return, I was forced to feel pain, anger, sadness, and guilt. And in these feelings came comfort. Anything would feel better than the nothingness.

Healing comes sitting in my parent's rocking chair, wrapped in a blanket, surrounded by my family. Healing comes at the wake, seeing his body, listening to stories, hugging friends, looking at photographs. Healing comes at the funeral, being in a crowded church, looking back at a never-ending procession of cars, standing before his plot surrounded by pine trees and green grass. Healing comes with phone calls and cards from friends.

Yet everyday I thought "no" and lived in slow motion. But time didn't really stop. As the days went on, I would look out the window and see people walking and cars moving. These strangers made me angry. How dare they go to the store. How dare the delivery boy march up to our house everyday and leave a newspaper. How dare the sun go down. And come up the next morning.

I returned to work later that week, unsure of how to "act," knowing my coworkers "knew". I divided them up into two categories. Those who asked so many questions they began to upset themselves, requiring my comfort. And those who never looked me in the face and never, ever mentioned "it".

The following week, I returned to school with the decision to tell no one. I needed the emotional haven. If no one knew about the death, I wouldn't have license to think, to feel, to grieve. I wouldn't have to worry if I was doing this right. After all, no one really teaches you how to mourn and be socially acceptable at the same time.

And then there are the dreams. I dreamt that Phil was alive and well and living at my parents' house. And the catch. He could remain alive and well, but could never leave my parents' house. Or the dream in which Phil could only be seen by my family, no one else. We were all experiencing similar dreams, bargains galore.

Time begins to speed up. The cards and phone calls come less frequently. The whole family comes down with a cold. The weather turns colder and the holidays are here. We enact our holiday traditions, marked by some tears, but mostly laughter. The traditions were familiar, down to the arrangement of the manger under the Christmas tree. It was easier with nothing left open for consideration.

January 15th. My mother stops by for a visit. "I think I'll have a dinner on Phil's birthday. Afterall, they held a memorial for Martin Luther King, Jr. and 100,000 people showed up."

January 27th. Phil's birthday complete with family, a dinner, and a birthday cake. We light the candles on the cake and sing happy birthday. Then there's a pause, maybe ten to fifteen seconds, until someone leans over and blows out the candles. I felt disappointed, hoping (thinking) that maybe Phil would blow out his own candles. My mother cut the cake and slices were passed around the table.

And still time endures. I used to cry several times a day. Then it was once a day, once a week, but never less than once a month. It gets a little darker a little earlier each evening. The leaves begin to change color. For some reason, this still surprises me.

September 25th. It's been one year since his death. I knew this date was coming. I could feel myself becoming melancholy, reflective, and irritable. I fight with my brother Mike about eating my last muffin. Together my family attends a mass at the church to which Phil belonged. The priest mentions his name in memory. I begin to cry and receive some stares from fellow church goers. They don't understand. But I'm not angry with them. I hope they never have the opportunity to understand. I apologize to Mike about the muffin scandal.

December 3rd. I'm down in Chicago with a friend getting what I perceive to be an early start on Christmas shopping. The phone rings. My brother Chris has been killed in a car accident. I knew what would happen next, how I would feel, what this meant. And yet I didn't."

* * *

What my daughter and I, and countless people before and since have discovered, is that our lives were never the same again. Grief moves us into a higher plane of existence in which we can love more intensely, suffer with more courage, and delve into life more spontaneously. The deeper we have descended into suffering, the higher we can soar into happiness. Your pain of grief is carving out a new place in your soul, and someday it can be filled with joy.

Footnotes

1 Michael Leming & George Dickinson, "Understanding Dying, Death, and Bereavement", Holt, Rinehart & Winston, Orlando, 1985, p.192..

2 Kenneth B. Schwartz Center, Massachusettes General Hospital, Boston, MA 02114-4724, Phone - 616-724-4746, Ellen Cohen, MSW President.

3 Elton John, "The Last Song", copyright Big Pig Music, 1992.

4 Sandol Stoddard, :The Hospice Movement", Random House, NY 1978, pp8,9.

5 Sandol Stoddard, "The Hospice Movement", Random House, NY 1978, pp. 254,255.

6 Dr. Elisabeth Kubler Ross, "On Death and Dying", Macmillan,NY, 1969.

7 Dr. Elisabeth Kubler Ross, "To Live Until We Say Goodbye", Prentice Hall, NJ.1978,pp100-101.

8 Dr. Elisabeth Kubler Ross, "To Live Until We Say Goodbye", Pentice Hall, NJ, 1978, pp48,57-58,72.

9 Dr. Elisabeth Kubler Ross,"To Live Until We Say Goodbye",Prentice Hall,NJ, 1978, pp114-117.

10 Marie Louise Von Franz, "Dreams & Death", Shambhala Press, Boston, 1986.

11 Dr. Elisabeth Kubler Ross, "The Wheel of Life", Scribner, NY,1997.

12 Raymond Moody,"Life After Life", Mockingbird Press,GA,1975.

Chapter Summaries

Chapter I. A Planned Departure. The death phobias of contemporary Western culture are learned behaviors absorbed as children from parents and adult role models. Before the age of eight, children who are exposed to death in a forthright manner are able to accept it fearlessly, as the natural end of all living things. Persons who have learned to accept the reality of death with a healthy attitude, can have a greater appreciation for life, and make better use of their time and the opportunities presented to them.

Advances in medical technology have enabled people with serious illnesses to survive for longer periods of time. Many who would have died suddenly are now revived by modern resuscitation methods. Some psychologists refer to this resulting interim of time as the stage of life devoted to the developmental task of dying.

The diagnosis of a life-threatening illness is received with varying degrees of acceptance or denial, depending on circumstances and personality. Time, careful consideration of personal desires, and a reasonable amount of research must be given to all decisions about physicians, diagnostic tests, treatments, and medical facilities to insure the best possible outcomes.

Chapter II. Living With a Life-Threatening Illness. The realization that medical intervention is not likely to cure a disease, drastically alters every aspect of the afflicted person's life. The most frequently asked question, "How long do I have?" cannot be answered with any degree of certainty due to each individual's will to live, and the unpredictability of the course of any disease. New coping strategies, and modifications in lifestyle can be learned, to insure the most vital and pleasurable living during this period.

Chapter III. How to Tell Others. Relationships are perceived to be altered by those who have a life-threatening illness. Eight major psychological and emotional blocks to honest comunication with friends and loved ones can be identified. These friends and family members find their own thoughts and feelings likewise altered. Understanding these communication blocks during times of serious illness, and learning new techniques to overcome them, makes openness of speech and actions possible. Honest communication allows love and bonding to grow during this time of crisis. The process, sometimes called anticipatory grief work, also eases final goodbyes should the illness result in death.

Chapter IV. Legal Loose Ends. A necessary, yet often disagreeable, task for those with a life-threatening illness, is the preparation of the legal documents which provide protection for themselves and their families. Necessary documents are: a Financial Power of Attorney if there is any possibility of becoming unable to handle customary monetary affairs; a Living Will, or Power of Attorney for Health Care stating which life-sustaining measures are desired; a Last Will and Testament, and an optional writing of bequest for smaller items of tangible property not listed in the Will; a Letter of Instruction containing any last wishes not previously documented, funeral arrangements, and the location and directions for important documents. Some may also want an Authorization to release medical information to their spouse or other, if they become unable to direct their care. Hiring an attorney is the easiest way to handle these legal papers, but this may be an additional financial burden. Pre-printed, fill-in-the-blank forms for most of these items are now available at hospital admitting desks, social service desks, and at office supply stores.

Chapter V. Getting Comfortable. One of the greatest fears of dying is the prospect of severe and lengthy periods of suffering. Modern pain management techniques, that can keep 98% of patients with severe and chronic pain comfortable, have been available for years. Many doctors and medical facilities do not make use of them, either through ignorance, cost cutting measures, or needless fears of making their patients drug addicted. Most patients still do not realize that their pain and symptoms can and should be kept under control. The psycho-social road blocks to pain management in both medical personnel and patients can be identified and discussed, and appropriate interventions initiated.

Chapter VI. Gathering Support. Aging and illness may progress to the point where assistance is needed to accomplish the activities of daily living. Most people in this position prefer to remain in their own homes. For home care it is possible to build a team of helpers from among friends and relatives, organize necessary tasks, cut down on the workload, and keep caregivers happy.

If there are children in the home they can be given simple tasks which make them feel they are part of the team. It is best to speak to them honestly about illness and dying, and reassure them that they are in no way to blame for the changes and sad feelings that may occur.

Those who have no family and friends to call on can contact a Home Care Nursing Service which has professional and trained personnel for all levels of care. Church and neighbor-hood volunteers are ready to help in many communities. If death is approaching, a Hospice Home Care Service or Inpatient Hospice is an excellent choice. Sources for financial help are also available.

Chapter VII. Your Rights. Those who endure prolonged bouts of illness frequently question their self worth and their right to burden others with their care. The root causes of these feelings need to be examined so that the unique worth of each individual can surface. A mutual gifting occurs as caregivers grow in understanding and love through sharing in this difficult experience.

In recent times a dying person's rights are thought to include the choice of suicide, with or without assistance. Those in favor of this right emphasize the quality of a person's life, those against it argue for the sanctity of human life. The "slippery slope" theory points to evidence that legalizing assisted suicide leads to widespread euthanasia. Improving the quality of to-day's pain control and healthcare for persons with long-term, incurable, or terminal illnesses, plays a vital role in curtailing the demand for assisted suicide.

Chapter VIII. Calming Emotional Storms. The internal and external adjustments that must be made during prolonged illness and the prospect of dying, cause many human emotions to erupt. At times they seem impossible to control or explain. Dr. Elisabeth Kubler-Ross found it helpful to classify them into five stages of grief: denial; anger; bargaining; depression; and acceptance. These do not usually follow in the order given but can appear at anytime during the illness, some more than once, and others not at all. Understanding and working through these emotions involves not only the sick person, but supportive friends, family, caregivers, and sometimes professional therapists.

Keeping pain and uncomfortable symptoms under control, and insuring proper rest and sleep, are essential in controlling emotional disturbances. The techniques of creative imaging, relaxation, exercise, verbalizing to a person or tape recorder, writing down thoughts and frustrations, and engaging in pleasurable activities are helpful. Dreams become more frequent as physical activities diminish, and dreams can play an important role in healing and calming emotions.

Chapter IX. Support Groups. A support group allows persons with similar diseases to join together for mutual sharing, caring, and learning from each other, usually with a group leader. Care should be taken to find a group with members in a similar stage of the same disease. Support groups can be beneficial enough to facilitate healing and sometimes effect cures. However, people should not let themselves be pressured into joining a certain group, or any group if they don't feel it is right for them.

Chapter X. Letting Go. The final stage of life, the developmental task of dying, consists of coming to terms with many losses, and re-evaluating goals, attitudes, and attachments. As physical possessions and pleasures are relinquished, many dying people experience an enhanced psychological and spiritual awareness which moves in to fill the void. These can subtly attract dying persons to an inner focus, which draws them away from events and persons around them. Any conflict of recent or past origin can interfere with this process as the person struggles to resolve the internal disturbance. Those who are closest to the person must also struggle to accept the final parting and let go of their loved one.

When death is near the person may begin to sleep most of the time. The body's functions begin to close down so that sense perceptions wane as does hunger and thirst. The sense of hearing may be present to the end.

Life after life experiences have been reported by hundreds of people, and many of the dying have found comfort in this glimpse of the next world. We may choose not to believe in these testimonies, but they do help to alleviate the fear of the unknown that death holds for all of us.

Chapter XI. For Those Left Behind. The wounds of grief are as serious as physical wounds and attention must be paid to their healing. The length of time needed for grieving varies greatly depending on circumstances and individual characteristics. It is wise to facilitate grief work through the many therapeutic sources available for those in mourning. Although occasional sadness and longing for the deceased person may occur throughout life, the grief process can be brought to a successful conclusion and joy can return. After moving past their grief, many people find they have developed more strengths and insights, and have cultivated a greater appreciation for life.

GLOSSARY

Acquired Immune Deficiency Syndrome (AIDS) - Gradual degeneration of the immune system caused by the Human Immunodeficiency Virus.

Acupressure - An ancient healing technique using pressure on selected nerves and blood vessels.

Acupuncture - A treatment for stress and pain relief in which needles are inserted into the skin and either manipulated or left for several minutes.

Amyotrophic Lateral Sclerosis (ALS) - also called Lou Gehrig's Disease. Progressive degeneration of the motor neurons resulting in loss of muscle activity and usually death within a few years.

Barbiturate - A sedative/hypnotic medication used to control convulsions and induce sleep.

Cardiopulmonary Resuscitation (CPR) - A method of restarting heart and lung functioning after they have ceased.

Catheter - A flexible tube used to withdraw liquid from any part of the body, or insert fluid into the body.

Catheter Irrigation - Method of preventing a catheter from clogging by injecting a small amount of fluid into the tubing.

Certified Home Health Aide - A person trained and certified by their place of employment to perform specific tasks.

Certified Hospice - Given approved status for meeting the requirements of the National Hospice Organization.

Congenital Anomalies - Any abnormal condition formed during gestation and present in the infant at birth.

Contracture - A permanent shortening and thickening of muscle fiber which prevents normal movement.

Down's Syndrome - A congenital chromosome disorder which causes mental retardation and Mongoloid facial features.

Durable medical equipment - Health care equipment that can be used repeatedly over a long period of time.

Durable Power of Attorney - A document which appoints a person to manage financial and every-day life affairs when the originator of the document is unable to do so.

Exacerbate - A condition in which a disease becomes more active and severe.

Financial Power of Attorney - Authorization of an appointed person to control another's monetary transactions. In this case attorney does not signify one who practices law.

Human Immunodeficiency Virus (HIV) - A virus which invades the host's cells and gradually causes the immune system's degeneration.

Huntington's Disease - An inherited, slowly progressive disease which is characterized by involuntary movements and mental retardation.

Hypertensive - A condition of having chronic high blood pressure. Also used to refer to medication used to control high blood pressure.

Kidney dialysis - A process which is the artificial equivalent to the natural clearance function of the kidneys.

Licensed Hospice Service - Organization caring for the dying which has been licensed by the state of occupancy.

Lymphoma - A type of malignant growth of the lymphoid tissue.

Mechanical ventilation - A device which artificially circulates air through the lungs when normal breathing has ceased.

Metastasis - A malignant growth that developed in one part of the body spreads to other tissues.

Multiple Sclerosis - A slowly progressing disease of the nervous system resulting in weakness and poor co-ordination.

Narcotic - An opium derivative or synthetic compound with similar properties used as medication to relieve severe pain.

Ostomy - A surgically formed artificial opening between a hollow organ and the abdominal wall.

Radiation - A therapy or treatment by either X-Ray or radioactivity used to destroy, shrink, or contain a malignant growth.

Reiki - An ancient form of therapy using the healing energy imparted by hands moving over the affected area of the body. Also employs healing mental energy.

Scope - also Endoscope - A thin tube-like instrument equipped with a light and lens to allow a physician to look into a body cavity.

Spina Bifida - A defective closure of the bony encasement of the spinal cord, formed in the infant during gestation.

Stigma - Any visible sign or blemish considered to be a mark of disgrace.

Viable - Condition of being normally capable of living.

DIRECTORY OF RESOURCES

AIDS

National Assn. of People with AIDS (NAPWA)
1413 K St. NW, Washington DC 20005
202-898-0414, Fax 202-898-0435
Email - napwa@napwa.org. , website www.napwa.org.
Monday - Friday 9a -5p EST & 24 hr. ans. service

National AIDS Hotline, Am. Social Health Assn.
PO Box 13827, Research Triangle Park, NC 27709
800-342-2437 (24 hrs.) / 800-243-7889 (TTY)
800-227-8922 for other sexually transmitted diseases
Information, counseling, referrals.

National Indian AIDS Hotline
PO Box 5370, Hopkins MN 55343, (800)283-2437
8:30a - 12 noon, 1p - 5p CST weekdays
Info pertinent to Indian community.

AIDS National Interfaith Network 800-288-9619
Info, support, guidance.

CDC National AIDS Clearinghouse
800-458-5231, 24 hr. ans. service and recorded msg.
M - F 9a-6p EST
Info, publications, personal guidance for all Socially
Transmitted Diseases (STD's)

HIV/AIDS Support Helpline
202-638-4200, 1101 14th St NW, Washington DC 20005
Fax 202-638-0243, www.pflag.org, e-mail: infoatpflag.org
M - F 9a - 3:30p EST, info & guidance

National Organization for HIV Over Fifty (NOHOF)
c/o Midwest AIDS Training and Education Center
808 S Wood St., MIC 779, Chicago IL 60612
312-996-1426, 24 hr. ans. service

Women Organized to Respond to Life-Threatening Diseases
WORLD: A newsletter by, for and about women
facing HIV disease. 414 13th St., 2nd floor, Oakland CA 94612
510-658-6930, 510-658-3040; Fax 510-658-3041, 24 hr ans.
M - F 10a - 6p PST; also website www.womenhiv.org

Immune Deficiency Foundation
Courthouse Square, 3565 Ellicot Mills Dr. Ellicot MD 21043
410-461-3127; Support structure for patients and their families
Info for professionals, patients, families.

CANCER

ACS, American Cancer Society
1599 Clifton Rd. NE, Atlanta GA 30329, 404-320-3333
website: http://www.cancer.org (serves all locations)
800-227-2345; 24 hr. ans.

ACS, Iowa Division
8364 Hickman Rd, Des Moines IA 50325, 515-253-0147

ACS, Minnesota Division
3316 W. 66th St, Minneapolis MN 55434, 612-925-2272

ACS, North Dakota Division
123 Roberts St, Box 426, Fargo ND 58107
701-232-1385,   Fax 701-232-1109

ACS, South Dakota Division
4101 Carnegie Pl. Sioux Falls, SD 57106-2322
800-660-7703

ACS, Wisconsin Division
N19W24350 Riverwood Dr., PO Box 902
Pewaukee, WI 53072-0902,   414-523-5500

Wisconsin Cancer Council - serving the Midwest
608-255-0058 weekdays 9a - 5p CST
Info, counseling, local referrals, connections with a variety of
resources.

American Institute for Cancer Research
1759 R St. NW Washington DC 20009
Nutrition Hotline 800-843-8114, 202-238-7744
Fax: 202-328-7726, M - F 9a - 5p EST
www.aicr.org/aicr
Info and guidance by Registered Dietitians on nutrition and
health questions. When you call, an operator will take your
question, your phone number and the best time for an AICR
nutritionist to return your call, usually within 24 hrs.

Cancer Information Service
800-4-CANCER, TTY 800-332-8615
 website http://rex.nci.nih.gov

Cancer Hope Network, 887-hopenet (467-3638)
2 North Road, Suite A, Chester NJ 07930
weekdays 9a - 5:30p EST, 24 hr. ans. service
www.cancerhopenetwork.org;
e-mail: info@cancerhopenetwork.org
Info on any cancer related problems, personal counseling
matches new cancer patients with experienced ones.

National Coalition for Cancer Survivorship
1010 Wayne Ave, 5th floor, Silver Spring MD 20910
888-650-9127. 301-650-8868, www.cansearch.org
e-mail: info@cansearch.org. Info and support after cancer
diagnosis by network of survivors.

Anderson Network
MD Anderson Comprehensive Cancer Center
Houston, TX , (800)-345-6324
connect with someone who has your same diagnosis

Bloch(Richard A.) Cancer Hot Line 800-433-0464
weekdays 9a - 4p CST
Counseling, sends free book, matches callers with similar
diagnosis.

Cancer Care, Inc
1180 Avenue of the Americas, 2nd floor, NY, NY 10036
800-813-HOPE (4673) 212-302-2400, www.cancercare.org
E mail: info@cancercare.org, Info, guidance by professionally
trained social workers, referral to local support, conference call
support groups.

National Ovarian Cancer Coalition
2335 E Atlantic Blvd. Suite 401,
Pompaneau Beach, Fla, 33062 (888)682-7426 (OVARIAN)
877-682-NOCC (6622) Fax 561-361-7655, M-F 9a - 5p EST
http://www.ovarian.org/
E-mail NOCC@ovarian.org

CONVERSATIONS!
Newsletter for Women who are fighting Ovarian Cancer
PO Box 7948, Amarillo, TX 79114-7948 (806) 355-2565
www.geocties/hotsprings/7938 e-mail: chmelanchon@aol,com

DES Cancer Network
514 10th St W Suite 400, Washington DC 20004-1403
800-337-6384   e-mail: desnetwork@aol.com
patient to patient support

Endometriosis Assn. International Headquarters
8585 N 76th Pl., Milwaukee WI 53223, 800-992-3036
www.endometriosisassn.org, 24 Hr. recording, free brochures
in all languages, may purchase books, tapes, and newsletters

ENCOREplus
YWCA of the USA, Office of Women's Health Initiative
624 9th St, NW, 3rd floor, Washington DC 20001-5394
Breast cancer info, exercise, & support   (800)953-7587
www.ywca.org   e-mail: hn2205@handsnet.org
local organizations in some cities.

Mothers Supporting Daughters with Breast Cancer
21710 Bayshore Rd., Chestertown MD 21620-4401
410-778-1982   Email - msdbc@dmw.com

National Alliance of Breast Cancer Organization
Nine East 37th St., 10th floor, NY,NY 10016
800-719-0154 website http://www.nabco.org/index/html
E-mail: nabcoinfo@aol.com Central resource for latest breast
cancer information.

Y-Me Breast Cancer Support Program
212 W. VanBuren, Chicago IL 60607 (800)221-2141
Spanish 800-986-9505 24 hr ans. service
www.y-me.org   e-mail: info@y-me.org
pre-surgery counseling, referrals, info, support

Look Good - Feel Better, American Cancer Society
800-395-look (5665) designed to help cancer patients improve
their appearance.

Alliance for Lung Cancer Advocacy, Support, Education
(ALCASE) 1601 Lincoln Ave, Vancover WA 98660
360-696-2436, 800-298-2436, www.teleport.com/alcase
E-mail: info@alcase.org

Lymphoma Foundation of America
PO Box 15335, Chevy Chase, MD 20825
800-500-9976, 202-223-6181
Info, support groups, patient advocacy.

Lymphoma Research Foundation of America, Inc.
8800 Venice Blvd, Suite 207, Los Angeles CA 90034
310-204-7040, website http://www.lymphoma.org
800-500-9976 E mail - Irfa@aol.com
Info, support, and national buddy system.

National Lymphedema Network
221 Post St. Suite 404, San Francisco CA 94115-3427
800-541-3259, 415-921-1306, Gives referrals for treatment
www.hooked.net/-lymphnet   e-mail: lymphnet@hooked.net
24 hr. ans. service takes names of callers and sends publications

S.P.O.H.N.C.
Support for People with Oral, Head, and Neck Cancer
PO Box 53, Locust Valley NY 11560-0053
516-759-5333, www.cybrmedical.com/spohnc.
E-mail: spohnc@ixnetcom.com
Patient run support group, newsletter, networking.

National Prostate Cancer Coalition
1300 19th St, NW, Suite 400, Washington DC 20036
813-253-0541, http://rattler.cameron.edu/npcc
Network of groups promoting education and research.

Prostate Cancer Support Network
300 W. Pratt St., Suite 401, Baltimore MD 21201
800-248-7866, nationwide network of support groups.

Us TOO, Inc. International
men with prostate cancer and their families
930 N York Rd. #50, Hillsdale, IL 60521
800-80USTOO (800-808-7866)
website http:/www.ustoo.com e-mail: ustoo@ustoo.com

OTHER RESOURCE ORGANIZATIONS

Air Care Alliance, National Patient Air Transport
PO Box 1940, Manassas, VA 20108-0804
Hotline 800-296-1217, charitable medical transport system

Air Life Line, 6133 Freeport Blvd., Sacramento CA 95822
800-446-1231, Fax 916-429-2166, http://www.airlifeline.org
E-mail staff@AirLifeLine.org 700 pilots provide nationwide
patient transportation.

American Brain Tumor Assn.
2720 River Rd, Suite 146, Des Plaines IL 60018
800-886-2282, Fax 847-827-9918 weekdays 9-5 CST
Info, Publications, referrals, counseling, support groups.

National Brain Tumor Foundation
785 Market St., Suite 1600, San Francisco CA 94103
800-934-CURE (2873) Info, support groups, referrals.

American Heart Assn.
7272 Greenville Ave, Dallas TX 75231-4596
214-373-6300

Am Heart Assn. - Iowa
1111 9th St, Suite 280, Des Moines IA 50314
515-244-3278

Am Heart Assn. - Minnesota
4701 W 77th St, Minneapolis, MN 55435
612-835-3300Am Heart Assn. - North & South Dakota
PO Box 1287, Jamestown ND 58402-1287
701-252-5122

Am Heart Assn - Wisconsin
795 N Van Buren, Milwaukee WI 53202
800-242-9236 weekdays 8:30-5 CST, Sends info.

Aplastic Anemia Foundation of America, Inc.
PO Box 22689, Baltimore MD 21203, (800)747-2820
www.aplastic.org   Info, counseling, resource referrals,
newsletters, supports worldwide research.

Bone Marrow Transplant
BMT Family Support Network 800-826-9376
PO Box 845, Avon CT 06001

BMT Newsletter
1985 Spruce Avenue, Highland Park, IL 60035
847-831-1913, Fax 847-831-1943

BMT Link Hotline - 800-LINK-BMT(546-5268)
29209 Northwestern Hwy. #624, Southfield MI 48034
Counseling, info, referrals.

Hospital Hospitality Houses, Inc.
National Assn. of "I Can Cope" Cancer Org.
(800)542-9730 www,vifit-usa.com/hhh e-mail: nahhhcom.com
call for low cost HHH in your locality; for patients undergoing
treatment and hospitalization away from home.

Huntington's Disease Society
140 W. 22nd St, 6th floor, NY, NY 10011-2420
800-345-4372, Speak with information specialist, newsletter,
sponsors nationwide events.

Impotence Information Center
10700 Bren Rd. West, Minnetonka, MN 55343
800-843-4315, weekdays 8:30 - 5 CST, 24 hr. ans. service
Info for treatment and cause of impotence.

Impotence World Association
10400 Little Patuxent Pkwy., Ste. 485, Columbia MD 21044
800-669-1603, 410-715-9605, Sends info on cause and
treatment. Referrals to specialized physician and
psychotherapist members. Self-help groups called "Impotents
Anonymous" and "I-Anon" for partners.

International Myeloma Foundation
2120 Stanley Hills Dr., Los Angeles, CA 90046
800-452-CURE (2873), www.myeloma.org
e-mail: theimf@aol.com   Hotline for info, treatment, and
management. Maintains patient to patient directory to provide
contact with others who share the same experiences.

Let's Face It
PO Box 29972, Bellingham, WA 98228-1972
360-676-7325 Support for facial disfigurement

National Foundation for Facial Reconstruction
317 E. 34th St., Room 901, NY,NY 10016 (800)422-3223
Physician, clinic, and hospital referrals. Assistance to those
unable to afford private care.

Leukemia Research Foundation
4761 W Touhy Ave., Suite 211
Lincolnwood, IL 60646 (847)982-1480
Info and financial aids to patients whose costs are not covered
by insurance or support groups. www.leukemia-research.org

Leukemia Society of America
600 Third Ave, 4th floor NY,NY 10016
800-955-4572, www.leukemia.org
 E-mail: frankbock@aol.com   Info, newsletters, referrals to
local support groups and programs.

Leukemia Society of Am - Wisconsin
1126 S 70th St., Suite N107B, West Allis, WI 53214
414-256-4020 Info, resources, and local referrals.

Lung Line, National Asthma Center
1400 Jackson St., Denver CO 80206, 800-222-5864
Weekdays 8 - 5 MST, RN's answer questions about asthma,
emphysema, smoking, allergies, and other respiratory disorders.

National Kidney Foundation
30 E. 33rd St., NY,NY 10016 (800)228-4483
Weekdays 9-5 EST, kidney disease info and referrals.

National Kidney Cancer Association
1234 Sherman Ave. Ste 203, Evanston IL 60602-1375
800-850-9132, 847-332-1051, Fax 847-332-2978
www.nkca.org   e-mail: office@nkca.org
Info to patients and physicians, patient advocacy.

National Association for Continence
PO Box 8310, Spartanburg SC 29305
(800)BLADDER (252-3337) Fax 803-579-7902
weekdays 8-5 EST Info, publications, quarterly newsletter with
membership ($20).

National Osteoporosis Foundation
1150 17th St, Ste. 500, Washington DC 20036
202-223-2226, weekdays 9-5 EST, 60 page handbook and
quarterly newsletter, Membership $15.00.

United Ostomy Association
36 Executive Park, Suite 120, Irvine CA 92714-6744
800-826-0826, www.uoa.org e-mail: uoa@deltanet.com
Weekdays 7:30 - 4:30 PST, Info, guidance, support.

National Center for Nutrition & Dietetics
American Dietetic Hotline
216 W. Jackson Blvd., Chicago IL 60606, www.eatright.org
800-366-1655 (24 hr recorded message) English & Spanish
To speak to a dietician call weekdays 9am and 4pm CST

National Institute of Mental Health
5600 Fisher's Lane, Room 7C-02, Rockville MD 20857
Depression Line 800-421-4211
Anxiety Disorders Info Line 888-269-4389
Panic Disorders Info Line 800-647-2642
Fax 301-443-5158, website http://www.nimh.nih.gov/
E mail - nimhninfo@nih.gov Daily recorded messages. English
& Spanish. 24 hrs.
                        AGING

AARP - American Assn. of Retired Persons (50 & over)
601 E Street, NW Washington DC 20049   www.aarp.org
Write for free publications on many supportive topics. A good
one to start with is "Staying in Charge"

National Institute on Aging Information Center
PO Box 8057, Gaithersburg MD 20898-8057
800-222-2225, TTY 800-222-4225
website http://www.nih.gov/nia/   niainfo@access.digex.net
Referrals to local Eldercare agencies & Eldercare Locator
to find suitable living arrangements if you must leave your home

Minnesota Board on Aging, Senior LinkAGE Line
444 Lafayette Rd North, St. Paul MN 55155-3843
800-333-2433, 616-296-2770 (after calling you will be asked to
enter your zip code - touchtone phone - to connect with group
in your area, for rotary phone, stay on the line for help.)

National Eldercare Institute on Health Promotion
601 E St. NW, Fifth Floor, Washington DC 20049
202-434-2220 Impliments programs for older adults, maintains
library of health info for seniors.

National Council on Aging
409 Third SW, 2nd Floor, Washington DC 20024
800-424-9046, weekdays 9-5 EST, info and publications on
senior employment, long term care, caregivers.

HOSPICE REFERRALS

National Hospice Organization
1901 N Moore St., Suite 901, Arlington VA 22209
800-658-8898 for local referrals and general information.
weekdays 9-5 EST
703-243-5990 for publications

North Dakota State Hospice Organization
St. Joseph's Hospital
30 W 7th St., Dickenson ND 58601, 701-225-7251

Minnesota State Hospice Organization
1619 Dayton Avenue, Suite 325, St. Paul, MN 55104
612-659-0423

Hospice Organization of Wisconsin
330 E. Lakeside, Madison WI 53715, 608-283-5418

BEREAVEMENT

Life Transitions Center, Inc.
3580 Harlem Rd., Buffalo, NY 14215-2045
(716) 836-6460,   Fax (716) 836-1578
Info, grief support programs.

Grief Recovery Institute
8306 Wilshire Blvd, Suite 21-A, Beverly Hills CA 90211
800-445-4808, www,grief-recovery.com Weekdays 9-5 PST
Counseling, support, info.

American Acadamy of Bereavement
Division of Carondelet Health Care
2090 North Kolb Rd., Suite 100, Tuscon, AZ 85715
520-721-3838, Info, professional training, resources.

CAREGIVERS

National Family Caregivers Association
10605 Concord St., Ste 501, Kensington MD 20895-3104
800-896-3650, 301-942-6430, www.nfccares.org
E-mail: info@nfccares.org, Info, education, counseling,
support groups, advocacy for caregivers.

Well Spouse Foundation
610 Lexington Ave, Ste. 814, NY, NY 10022-6005
(800)838-0879, 212-644-1241, Info and guidance for well
spouse of a chronically ill person, newsletter, local support
groups, "round robin" letter writing, bereavement counseling.

COMPLEMENTARY THERAPY

Biological Remedies, 512-926-4900 or website:
www.herbalgram.org

Resource for publications about complementary and alternative
medicine research supported by NIH (National Institute of
Health): OAM Clearinghouse - Office of Alternative Medicine,
National Institute of Health, P O Box 8218,
Silver Spring, MD 20907-8218, 888-644-6226.

INDEX

ORDER FORM

Please send _____ copy/copies of **Time To Say Goodbye** to:

Name_____

Address_____

City_____**State,Zip**_____

Price: . . . . . $14.95 per copy* $_____
Shipping: . . . $3.95 for the first and
                $1.00 for each additional book $_____

                          TOTAL $_____

Kindly enclose a money order or check with your order, or:
*Mastercard*_____ *Visa*_____Acct. No._____
Expiration date _____Authorized Signature _____

mail to: **Lemieux International, Ltd.**
P. O. Box 17134
Milwaukee, Wisconsin 53217-0134
or call: **1-800-950-7723**. - e-mail - barbrolive@aol.com
with questions or comments; visit our website at:
www.galaxymall.com/time to say goodbye

*Quantity Purchases: We offer a discount price, ($10/per book) on the purchase and shipping of five or more copies for educational or medical distribution. (S&H: 5 books/$6 --10/$8)

Yes! The charcoal sketches are available - 20"x 24" copies suitable for framing @ $20 each, plus $4 shipping 1 to 3 copies. Order by chapter name or number.